Seniors Guide to Iphone & Macbook:
The Most Easy to Follow and Intuitive Guide
to Master Your iPhone and MacBook with
Best Tips and Instructions.

.

CONTENTS:

Introduction

We have combined two books into one in order to bring more benefits to the elderly. iPhone and Macbook are two devices that complement each other, so this book contains all the most valuable instructions for you.

One of the most talked-about topics in the IT world is whether iPhones are better than Android smartphones or vice versa. Android users sometimes complain that iPhone users are just concerned about branding. On the other hand, Android supporters say Android smartphones contain too complicated, unworkable features.

However, purchasing a cellphone should go beyond personal preferences. Although both have advantages and disadvantages, one operating system beats the other in certain areas.

So, if you've been considering purchasing a new iPhone, we've compiled a list of all the ways iOS outperforms Android to help you make an educated decision.

Benefits of iPhone:

- Maintains its market value
- Reduced Security Risks
- The interface is really user-friendly.
- Superior Phone Security Plans
- Apple Ecosystem Is Seamlessly Integrated
- Fakes are Simple to Recognize
- Natural-Looking Photos and a Functional Camera
- Quick Updates
- Apple Pay is easier to use.
- Third-Party Apps Perform Better on iPhones

If you want a user-friendly, uncomplicated gadget that requires no technical understanding, get a new iPhone. You'll appreciate Apple's ecosystem.

If you prefer a more customized, open platform, you might want to investigate devices that operate on Android operating systems. Don't forget that there are plenty of Android manufacturers to pick from.

Overall, don't restrict your options. Based on your lifestyle, technological proficiency, and device preferences, consider how an iOS or Android smartphone will benefit you.

Using a Mac is straightforward. In fact, they are regarded as more user-friendly than Windows computers. But there is a learning curve if you've never used one before, especially if you're accustomed to Windows.

Part 1: iPhone for Seniors

Chapter 1: Starting UP with iPhone

Overview of your iPhone

iPhone, series of cellphones manufactured by Apple Inc. that combine mobile phone, digital camera, music player, and personal computer features. In 2007, after more than two years of research, the gadget was introduced for the first time in the United States. Europe and Asia subsequently received the iPhone in 2007 and 2008, respectively.

Apple's first mobile smartphone was built to run the Mac OS X operating system, which was popularized on the company's personal computers. The most innovative aspect of the gadget was its touch-sensitive multisensor interface. Instead of a pen or physical keyboard, the touchscreen enabled users to operate all applications and telephone features with their fingers. This interface—perfected, if not developed, by Apple—recreated a tactile physical experience; for instance, the user may reduce the size of photographs by pinching or browse through music albums by flicking. Additionally, the iPhone had Internet access, music and video playing, a digital camera, visual voicemail, and a contact list with tabs.

The iPhone joined a crowded market for smartphones, and both critics and enthusiasts noticed that it provided few really novel features. The iPhone's key selling point was its combination of user-friendly software and an attractive, streamlined interface, as well as its ability to integrate new user-selected applications. In the first 60 days after Apple opened its online iPhone App Shop in 2008, more than 100 million programs (or "apps") were downloaded, and by January 2010, more than three billion apps had been downloaded from the store.

In 2008, less than a year after the iPhone's introduction, Apple introduced a second model that utilized third-generation (3G) cellular technology. As was the case with the first iPhone, the new iPhone 3G sold one million devices in its first three days on the market. In addition to hardware upgrades including as a 3-megapixel digital camera that could also capture digital movies and an integrated digital compass (compatible with many mapping applications), the iPhone 3GS had a new operating system, iPhone OS 3.0. The new system included voice-activated controls and peer-to-peer (P2P) play of electronic games through Wi-Fi Internet connections with other iPhone users. The latter feature was part of Apple's attempt to compete with the Nintendo Company's DS and the Sony Corporation's PSP in the portable gaming industry.

Turning on and turning off your phone

Turn on or off iPhone:

- Utilize the side button to activate iPhone. To switch off iPhone, use the side button (together with either volume button on some models) or Settings.
- If your iPhone is not functioning as intended, you may restart it by turning it off and then on again. If turning it off and back on does not resolve the problem, try forcing a restart.

Hold the side button in place until the Apple logo shows.

To turn off an iPhone with Face ID, press and hold the side button and either volume button simultaneously until the sliders display, then move the Power Off slider.

- iPhone equipped with a Home button: Hold the side button while dragging the slider.
- All models: Navigate to Settings > General > Shut Down, and then adjust the slider.

Apple ID

Apple ID administration is crucial to the Apple experience. Each individual must utilize their own Apple ID for iCloud, Messages, and FaceTime. People in the same home or small group can simultaneously share an Apple ID for music and applications. Discover how to enter your Apple ID into applications.

Ensure that each user has a unique Apple ID for iCloud, Messages, and FaceTime. If you configure iCloud for many users with the same Apple ID, their contacts and calendars, notes and reminders, photographs and documents will be identical. If you share an Apple ID for Messages and FaceTime, you will also get each other's text messages and video calls.

Connect all of your email accounts to your Apple ID. How will others discover you to send you a text message, make a FaceTime call, or share iCloud calendars or picture streams if your primary email address is different from your Apple ID, or if you have multiple email addresses? Therefore, it is imperative that you link all of your major email accounts to your Apple ID. You may do so through the Messages or FaceTime settings, or by logging into Apple ID on the web (see below).

We suggest utilizing Family Sharing for applications, music, and movies for your home or small team. You may share your purchases with this account, but you will only be charged once.

If a user purchases an app or media using their own Apple ID, it is theirs or the Family Sharing group's. You cannot update applications or move applications or media assets to a different account. Even if a different individual is using the same equipment, you will need to repurchase applications and media.

Apple identifies purchases using an Apple ID. Every purchased music, book, film, and application is associated with the Apple ID used to make the transaction. This Apple ID and associated password are required to move purchases to a new device or update an application. If you have many Apple IDs, there will be far more to monitor. And sadly, Apple IDs cannot be consolidated. After using an Apple ID, there is no turning back.

You may simplify your life by utilizing only one of your Apple IDs for future transactions, while being unable to merge or terminate accounts. If you have iTunes Match, you should now utilize that Apple ID. Otherwise, utilize the Apple ID with the greatest number of transactions. Discover how to examine your buying history.

If you are experiencing trouble keeping track of your Apple IDs or locating the correct applications, music, contacts, and calendars, please contact us. We are here to assist.

Where may an Apple ID be used?

Use your Apple ID to purchase music and movies in iTunes, ringtones, books and magazines on your iPhone, iPad, or iPod touch, and software for your Mac, as well as to access your music in the cloud with iCloud Music Library and iTunes Match. An Apple ID is the foundation for iCloud, which synchronizes your contacts, calendars, photographs, passwords, and documents across all of your Apple devices. Game Center, FaceTime, and iMessage all require an Apple ID. Find My Friends, My iPhone, My iPad, and My Mac require it. Apple ID enables Home Sharing, which allows you to link your devices with an Apple TV or transfer music between computers. Access and synchronize Photos with iCloud Photo Library. Take a course through iTunes U. You may use your Apple ID to log onto a Mac. Use your Apple ID to make Genius Bar reservations at an Apple Retail Store. You may also purchase Apple products at www.store.apple.com and monitor your AppleCare warranty or Apple support online. Simply said, your single Apple ID should be used for all Apple-related activities across all of your devices.

Home Screen

There are several ways to utilize an iPhone. You may equip your iPhone with a trackpad keyboard and use it as a PC. Alternatively, you can now add widgets to your iPhone to personalize it. In both circumstances, the correct home screen is required. Knowing where everything is kept, making your own folders, and even having the appropriate wallpaper may alter how you use and operate your iPhone.

You may believe you know everything there is to know about the home screen, but there is much more to discover. Siri, the Today View, and the Control Center are included. Especially today, when iOS 14 have introduced so many new features, there have never been more things to try. Here is all you need to know in order to master the home screen on your iPhone! To return to home screen you need simply press the Home button or swipe up from the central bottom part (virtual home button).

The home screen of an iPhone is not intended to be a destination or a location to spend time or put widgets. It is intended to serve as a hub for all your apps, both native and those downloaded through the App Store. The Home screen is where everything begins, regardless of how you access apps: by exploring Home screen pages, by searching with Spotlight, by jumping directly to activities with 3D Touch or Haptic Touch, or by using Siri.

Language settings

If you want to change the language on your iPhone, just follow our quick and straightforward instructions.

There are several reasons why you may wish to alter the iPhone's system language. For starters, it might be set to the wrong language, making the whole thing hard to understand. For instance, you may speak more than one language and wish to change the phone's language. This chapter demonstrates step-by-step how to change your iPhone's language, regardless of your cause or requirement.

What we applied

- The Condensed Version
- Launch the Options app
- Continue down to General
- Select Language and Country
- Select iOS Language
- Select your native tongue from the list.

Step 1

Launch your iPhone's Settings application. This symbol resembles a mechanical gear.

Step 2

Continue down to General

Once within the Settings menu, navigate to the General section and hit it.

Step 3

Select Language and Region from this menu.

Step 4

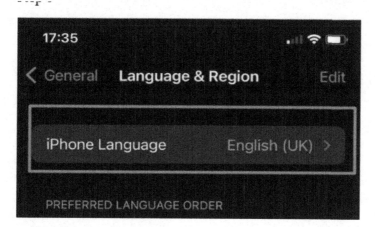

Select the iPhone language.

Step 5

Select your language from the list, then confirm your selection.

Now a list should display, giving you the choice to change your iPhone's language. Select your preferred language and confirm your selection.

Touch ID and Face ID

The Touch ID or Face ID capabilities on your iPhone or iPad are an excellent way to strike a balance between ease and security. Learn how to configure and utilize Touch ID or Face ID to keep your iOS device safe.

Apple has made Touch ID and Face ID, which are two ways to unlock iOS devices securely without having to type in a PIN or passcode every time.

While the business still requires customers to use a numeric PIN or alphanumeric PIN code to lock their devices, it has made the Touch ID and Face ID technologies available to provide the optimal mix of security and convenience.

Why is Touch ID used?

Touch ID is a feature on iPhones, iPads, and iPod touches from Apple that lets the user's fingerprint be used as proof of identity. Instead of manually entering a PIN or password, users may unlock their iOS devices by resting their finger on the Touch ID hardware. Touch ID also allows you to make purchases on the App Store and iTunes Store, authenticate your identity for Apple Pay purchases, and much more.

Apple can store up to five unique fingerprints, so if multiple people want to, they can share access to a device. Touch ID unlocks are quick and simple to configure. Let's examine how to configure and utilize Touch ID on an iPhone or iPad.

Configuring and Using Touch ID on an iPhone or iPad

Configuring Touch ID on an iPhone or iPad is a simple, one-time operation. In less than five minutes, you can enable Touch ID and take the first step in securing your iPhone or iPad. But first, you must determine which iPhone or iPad model you currently own.

If you possess any of the aforementioned gadgets, congrats! Touch ID may be configured and used on your smartphone. The Touch ID hardware is integrated into your device's home button, so each time you press the home button, you touch the Touch ID hardware. Here are instructions for configuring and using Touch ID on an iPhone or iPad.

1. Launch the Settings app on your iOS device.
2. Select Touch ID & Passcode by navigating down a bit.
3. If a password or PIN is presently configured on your iOS device, you will be asked to enter it.
4. Before you can set up Touch ID, you must generate a passcode if you do not already have one. To continue, tap the Turn Passcode On option.
5. Tap "Add a Fingerprint" next. The gadget requests that you place your finger on the home button and lift it when you hear a beep.
6. Keep lifting and putting down your finger so the Touch ID hardware can read it.
7. After completion, proceed to Adjust Your Grip. This scans the edges of your fingers so that the gadget has a complete fingerprint reading.
8. Your fingerprint has now been registered on your iPhone or iPad.

You may now use the fingerprint you created to unlock your iPhone or iPad. In addition, you may make transactions with your fingerprint. Here's how to make purchases on an iPhone or iPad using Touch ID.

How to Enable Touch ID Purchases on an iPhone or iPad:

After setting up Touch ID on your iOS device, you may use it to authenticate your identity while making purchases from the App Store, iTunes Store, Apple Books, etc. This is how:

- Launch the Settings app on your iOS device.
- Select the Touch ID & Passcode option by scrolling down.
- Enable the toggle for iTunes & App Store. This may require logging into your iTunes or App Store account.
- Your smartphone will now prompt you to Pay with Touch ID anytime you attempt to buy or download an item from the App Store or iTunes Store.

What exactly is Face ID?

Beginning with the release of iPhone X, Apple has replaced the Touch ID function in iPhones with Face ID. Face ID, as the name indicates, enables a user to unlock their iOS device using their face as the authentication method. Face ID, according to Apple, is a superior and more secure technology than Touch ID and offers several benefits. Face ID hardware is comprised of an array of cameras and sensors located above the iPhone displays, as opposed to the Touch ID hardware that resides in the Home Button at the bottom.

Face ID: Does my iPhone have it?

Face ID was introduced with the iPhone X in 2017 for the first time. Since then, Apple has introduced more iPhones and iPads with Face ID hardware, allowing you to unlock iOS devices and make payments with Face ID. The following iPhones and iPads use Face ID:

- iPhone X iPhone XS are the iPhone models featuring Face ID.
- Max iPhone XS

- Apple iPhone XR
- iPad Pro is a list of iPads with Face ID (3rd Generation, 2018)

Face ID Configuration and Use on iPhone

Enabling and setting Face ID on an iPhone or iPad is a straightforward procedure. By following this easy-to-understand guide to setting up Face ID on iOS devices, you can start using it in minutes to unlock your iPhone or iPad. This is how:

- Launch the Settings app on your iOS device.
- Face ID & Passcode may be accessed by selecting the Face ID & Passcode option. If asked, enter the passcode for your device to proceed.

- Tap Configure Face ID.

- Hold your smartphone upright in Portrait position around 10 to 20 inches in front of your face.

- Tap the Get Started button to continue.

- Position your face within the circular frame preview and complete the circle by slowly moving your head in a round motion.
- Tap Continue once the first scan is complete.

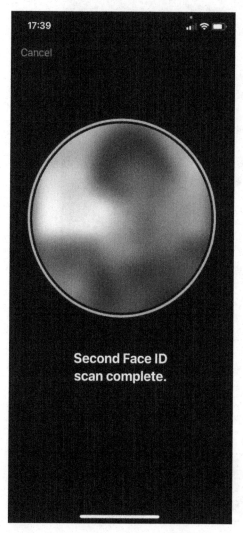

- Repeat the directions in Step 6 on a second occasion.
- Once you have finished the steps, tap Done.

If you have not yet set up a passcode for your iOS device, you must do it immediately so that you have an alternative to Face ID in the event that it fails to detect your face.

How to Make Purchases on an iPhone or iPad Using Face ID

After setting up and configuring Face ID on your iOS device, you may use it not just to unlock the device but also to make purchases from iTunes and App Stores. To enable Face ID purchases on your own iPhone or iPad, follow these easy steps:

- Launch the Settings app on your iOS device.
- Face ID & Passcode may be accessed by selecting the Face ID & Passcode option. Enter your device passcode to continue.
- Enable the switch for iTunes & App Store, Apple Pay, and Password Autofill in the list of toggles under USE FACE ID FOR.
- To confirm, you may be required to enter your App Store password.

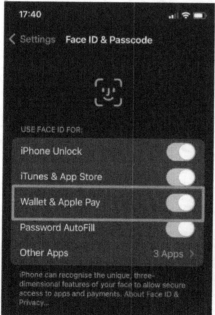

-
- Double-clicking the sleep/wake button on the side of the iPhone or iPad will now authenticate purchases using Face ID anytime you make a transaction.

Keyboard Size and languages

There are several ways to increase the size of the iPhone's keypad. For the first, you have to change the iPhone's display settings. For the second, you have to switch to a different keyboard app.

Even though the iPhone doesn't have a way to make the keyboard bigger, it does have a Display Zoom feature that can make any part of the screen bigger, including the keyboard. Here's how to turn it on.

- Launch the iPhone's Settings app and navigate to Display & Brightness.

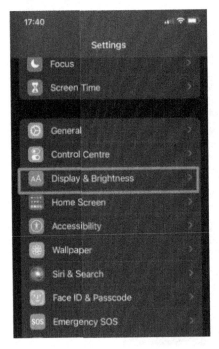

- In the Display Zoom section, touch the View button. Now, change the view type to Zoomed and hit the Set button in the upper right corner.

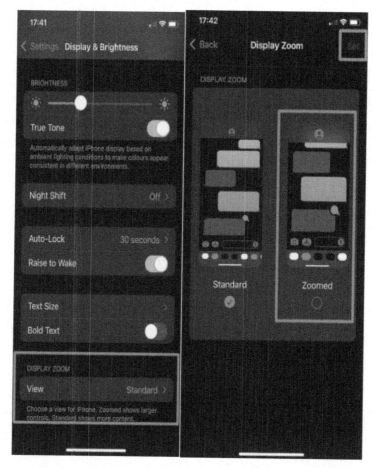

- Your iPhone will go back to the new zoom level, and everything, including the text, icons, and keyboard, will be bigger than before.

How to Reduce the iPhone Keyboard

If you have little hands like mine and are using one of the bigger iPhone models, the default keyboard may occasionally feel too big.

The easiest way to make your iPhone keypad smaller is probably to turn on the "one-handed mode." This is how.

- To start the keyboard, run any program that uses the keyboard, such as messaging.

- Select the left- or right-handed layout by pressing and holding the globe symbol below the keyboard.

That is all. Now, the size of the keyboard on your iPhone will remain the same, but the keys will decrease, making it simpler to type with one hand.

How can I change the iPhone keyboard's language?

Approximately 80 different languages are installed on the iPhone keyboard. You can switch to any of these languages by going to Settings > General > Keyboard > Keyboards > Add New Keyboard. Select a new language from the drop-down menu and then press

Done.

You can hide or expand the iPhone keyboard by swiping your finger down from above the text entry field.

If you are using the normal iPhone keyboard, the Settings app allows you to remove the keyboard history. To accomplish this, head to General > Reset > Reset Keyboard Dictionary and select Reset Dictionary.

Connecting to WIfi

Whether you're setting up your iPhone for the first time or need to connect to a new network, learning how to locate and connect to a specific Wi-Fi network is a crucial step. Wi-Fi enables users to connect to the internet through a router or network without utilizing cell phone data.

All iPhone generations are capable of connecting to Wi-Fi. No matter if you're trying to connect to a public, private, or hidden Wi-Fi network, it's easy and can be done in a few minutes. Here is the procedure.

- Launch Settings, as shown on an iPhone X.

-

- Go to the Wi-Fi option in the Settings menu and press it.
- Find Wi-Fi in your settings.

-
- Ensure that the Wi-Fi button is on before proceeding (if it is, the slider will appear green).
- Ensure that your Wi-Fi is on.
- Tap the name of the Wi-Fi network to which you wish to join.

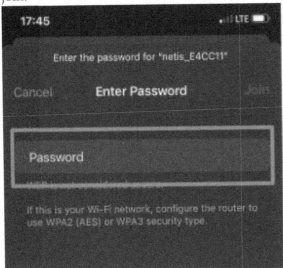

-
- Enter the password for the Wi-Fi network that was selected.
- Input the passphrase
- In the top right corner, tap Join.

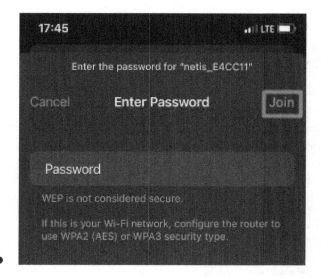

Sound Settings

Change the noises iPhone plays when you receive a call, text, voicemail, email, reminder, or other sort of notification by navigating to Settings.

On devices that feature haptic feedback, you feel a tap after performing certain operations, like as touching and holding the Camera icon on the Home Screen.

- Navigate to Settings > Sounds and Haptics.
- Drag the slider underneath Ringtone and Alert Level to adjust the volume of all sounds.
- Tap a sound type, such as a ringtone or text tone, to adjust the tones and vibration patterns for sounds.

-
- Perform any of the following:
- Choose a pitch (scroll to see them all).

-
- Text tones are used for text messages, fresh voicemail, and other notifications. Ringtones are used for incoming calls, clock alarms, and the clock timer.

- Tap Vibration, then choose a vibration pattern that's already there or tap Create New Vibration to make your own.
- You may also modify the sounds that the iPhone plays for certain individuals. Go to Contacts, tap the name of a contact, click Edit, and then choose a ringtone and a text tone.
- Toggle haptic feedback on or off.
- On compatible models, go to Settings > Sounds & Haptics.
- Switch System Haptics on or off.

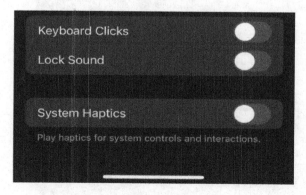

- When System Haptics is off, you will not hear or feel incoming calls and notifications.

If you aren't getting calls and notifications when you should, go to the Control Center and check if Do Not Disturb is turned on. Tap it if it is highlighted to disable Do Not Disturb. (When Do Not Disturb is on, the status bar will also indicate this.

Notifications Preferences

As part of iOS, push notifications are enabled by default. Choose the applications from which you wish to get notifications and the sort of alerts they deliver.

- To enter the Settings app, tap its icon.
- To view the applications installed on the device that allow notifications, tap Notifications.
- Select Show Previews and decide when alerts will appear.

-

- Receive alerts when the phone is locked or unlocked at all times.

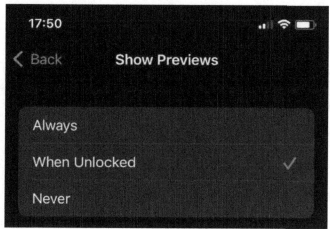

- When unlocked, the lock screen does not display notifications. Select this option to minimize disruptions and preserve your privacy.
- Alerts do not appear on the phone ever.
- In the Notifications settings, tap the app whose settings you want to change, then tap the Allow Notifications switch to see the app's notification options.
- Turn off Allow Alerts if you do not wish to receive push notifications from the app.
- In the Alerts section of iOS 12, pick the desired alert kind. A checkmark displays next to the active options.
- Alerts display on the lock screen when the phone is locked.
- Notification Center: Alerts are stored in the Notification Center, which may be accessed via the Lock Screen or by sliding down from the top of the display.
- To change the duration of a notification's display, hit Banner Style (or, in iOS 11, tap Show as Banners). Then select an option:
- These alerts are persistent: they remain on the screen until you tap or dismiss them.

Airdrop

AirDrop allows you to send and receive photos, documents, and other files with nearby Apple devices. For contacts, they must adjust their AirDrop reception option to Everyone for the file to be received.

AirDrop reception settings may be modified to Contacts Only or Off at any time to manage who can see your device and send you content over AirDrop.

You may also utilize AirDrop between Apple devices. If the AirDrop button has a red number on it, it means that you can share with more than one device nearby. Tap the AirDrop button, followed by the individual with whom you wish to share.

If the individual with whom you're sharing content is in your Contacts, their image will appear next to their name. If they are not in your contacts, their name will appear without a picture.

How to utilize AirDrop

When someone shares anything with you via AirDrop, you receive a notification that includes a Use the same motion to get to Control Center on an iPad with iOS 12 or later, or iPadOS. Use the same motion to get to Control Center on an iPad with iOS 12 or later, or iPadOS. Swipe up from the bottom of the display on your iPhone 8 or before.

- Touch and hold or press firmly on the network settings card in the upper-left corner.
- Touch and hold the AirDrop button, then select from the following options:
- Receiving Credit: You will not accept requests through AirDrop.

- Only your contacts have access to your smartphone.
- Everyone: All adjacent Apple devices that are AirDrop-enabled can see your device.
- If you can't change Receiving Off by tapping:
- Go to Screen Time in Settings.
- Tap content restrictions and privacy settings.
- Tap Allowed Applications and ensure that AirDrop is enabled.

Chapter 2: iPhone Screen Settings

Changing Wallpaper

Changing your phone's wallpaper is one of the least expensive methods to customize its appearance without purchasing extra accessories such as phone covers or grips. It's also a great way to display images of your family, friends, pets, vacation pictures, or anything else you want to view every time you pick up your smartphone.

Apple permits iPhone users to choose their home screen and lock screen independently, allowing them to pick two separate images as their wallpaper, or the same image for both screens. Currently, the majority of iPhones also enable Live wallpapers, so you can set one that moves and comes to life when you tap and hold the screen.

What is required:

- Access the phone's settings.
- Tap Wallpaper Tap Select a New Background
- Select a folder
- Choose a picture
- Tap Set Touch Set Home Screen, Touch Set Lock Screen, or Touch Set Both.

How to change the background on your iPhone

- First, access your phone's settings.
- Tap Wallpaper

- You might have to scroll down to locate this option.
- Tap Select a New Background

- At this point, you may also touch on any of your current wallpapers to reposition or resize them.

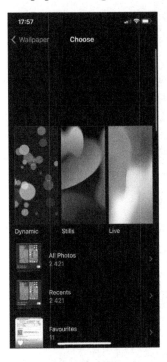

- Choose a folder
- To utilize an image from your Photos, you may choose between Apple's collections of Dynamic, Still, and Live photos or one of your own folders.
- Tap the desired background picture
- Move or resize the picture by clicking and dragging the mouse Set
- The picture may be moved by dragging it or scaled by pinching it with two fingers.
- Determine where you will place the wallpaper.
- You have the option of setting it as your lock screen, your home screen, or using the same picture for both.

Screen Brightness

Your iPhone or iPad is quite adept at changing the screen's brightness based on its surroundings. Occasionally, you may need to perform this action manually. Here's how to alter the iPhone or iPad's screen brightness.

You may adjust the screen brightness from either the Control Center or the Settings app.

Swipe down from the screen's upper-right corner on an iPhone or iPad to access the Control Center. If the Home button is present on your iPhone, slide up from the bottom.

You'll find the Sun icon/Brightness slider adjacent to the Sound icon/Volume slider.

Drag the slider up or down to raise or decrease the brightness.

To have additional control, extend the brightness bar by pressing and holding it. A far larger slider will show up as well as choices to enable Dark mode and Night Shift. Again, swipe up or down to adjust the brightness of the display.

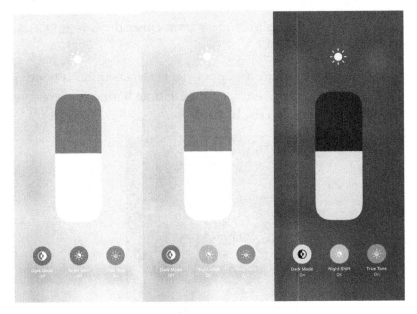

To return to the Control Center after adjusting the screen brightness to your liking, tap the empty space outside the slider.

Alternately, screen brightness may be adjusted via the "Settings" app. Simply press the Gear symbol to access "Settings," then tap "Display and Brightness"

- Drag the "Brightness" slider to the left or right to adjust the brightness level.
- As long as you remain in the same surroundings, the brightness will remain constant. If the Auto-Brightness option is turned on, however, the brightness will change automatically based on the amount of light in the area (and

the amount of battery life left) when you move to a new place.

- You can turn off Auto-Brightness if you want to have full control over the brightness of the screen.
- To accomplish this, launch the "Settings" app and tap "Accessibility."
- Select "Display & Text Size"
- To disable this function, go down and select "Off" from the "Auto-Brightness" option.

Now, it will not change automatically until you explicitly adjust the brightness.

Folders for applications

If you possess an iPhone, you have probably downloaded several applications. Creating folders on your iPhone's Home Screen is one of the finest methods to arrange these applications. You may rely on the App Library to manage your iPhone apps, but establishing your own folders provides you far more power. And it takes only a second to create one.

So, if you don't know how to make a folder on an iPhone, this guide will show you how.

- Create a Folder for Apps on an iPhone
- Before you can create a folder on your iPhone, you must tap and hold the Home Screen.

- This will cause your applications to jiggle, and you'll be given the opportunity to uninstall any you don't want.
- Now, by dragging one app on top of another, an iPhone folder will be automatically created.

- Once a folder has been created, you may add and delete as many applications as you wish. You may also create an unlimited number of folders.
- When you start organizing your iPhone apps, you might want to put your pictures in albums and folders.

●

How to Delete or Rename an Application Folder

If you wish to rename a folder containing apps on your iPhone, open the folder in question and look at the top. There, you will find the folder's current name. Simply hold down the name with your finger to alter it. Alternatively, you may press and hold the folder before tapping Rename.

The option to modify this folder will then become available. Simply replace the current name with the desired folder name. You may alternatively create an empty folder.

If you wish to delete a folder, you may drag all of its applications out of it, and the folder will be deleted automatically. You may also opt to remove the folder from the Home Screen; however, this will also remove the applications from the Home Screen and place them in the App Library. If this is what you intend to accomplish, then good for you.

Chapter 3: Making Photo with iPhone

How to make photos

As with many other iPhone apps, the Camera app icon is located on the Home screen. The Camera app is located on the upper row of icons, all the way to the right and next to its relative, the Photos symbol, unless you relocated it.

You might as well take a photo now:

- Tap the Camera icon on the Home screen. Or, from the Lock screen, double-tap the Home button and then swipe the Camera symbol in the lower-right corner of the display upward.

 o
- These activities essentially transform the iPhone into a Kodak Instamatic, sans the film, of course.

- Maintain your focus on the iPhone's display.

  o
- On the screen, the first thing you see is something resembling a closed camera shutter. However, this shutter opens in roughly a second on the iPhone 4 and in a snap on the iPhone 4S and 5, displaying what the camera lens sees.
- Using the iPhone's display as a viewfinder, aim the camera toward the subject you wish to photograph.

Ensure that the switch in the lower-right corner of the screen is set to camera mode, not video mode.

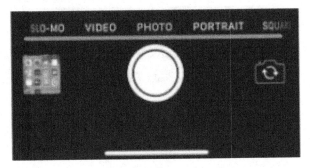

(The switch displays in the upper-right corner of the screen when the iPhone is oriented in landscape mode.) The on-screen button is located beneath the image of a camera rather than the image of a video camera.

When you're pleased with what's in the frame, you may take a photo by doing one of the following:

- To take a picture, tap the camera-shaped icon at the bottom of the screen. The camera icon is on the right when the iPhone is held horizontally. If required, you will be able to shift the point of concentration.

- Try this technique if you have difficulties keeping the camera steady. Instead of tapping the camera symbol at the bottom of the screen, keep your finger held to it and only release it when you are ready to take a picture.

- The volume up button is pressed. This method of photography is superior since it replicates the sensation of using a conventional camera. However, if you are an iPhone purist, continue to utilize the on-screen camera button.

- You may encounter temporary shutter lag on the iPhone 4, so make careful to remain motionless. On the iPhone 4S and 5, shutter latency is no longer an issue due in part to their faster processors. When the shutter reopens, the captured image is briefly visible. The screen works as a viewfinder once more so that the next image may be captured.

If the iPhone is held horizontally when taking a picture, the image is stored in landscape orientation.

The iPhone's on-screen camera button is hypersensitive. A simple tap is all that is necessary to capture an image.

Basic settings of your camera

Think you know everything there is to know about the iPhone camera? Possibly so, if you are a skilled photographer who enjoys tinkering with camera settings. There is always something new to learn about photography for everyone else.

Continue reading if you'd want to become an expert iPhone user. We will expose you to numerous iPhone camera settings to help you take the images.

Preserve Settings

Do you have a favorite camera mode or custom filter? If so, it's annoying to have to choose it again each time you use the Camera app. By the time you set up your camera, the ephemeral moment you wanted to record may have already disappeared.

Open the Settings app and scroll to Camera > Preserve Settings to configure it. There are many settings to choose from, such as Camera Mode, Creative Controls, Exposure Adjustment, Night Mode, and Live Photo.

Apple provides brief explanations beneath the options if you are confused of what they relate to if the options differ slightly based on the iPhone model you have.

Activate Grid Lines

The Rule of Thirds is something that most people who like photography are familiar with. It's one of the most important rules to follow when putting together a shot. Simply put, it specifies that the subject of a photograph should be placed at one of the four intersections of lines on a 3x3 grid.

To get the most out of this rule, you must activate an on-screen grid in your iPhone's camera settings so that you can see the four intersections. Also, gridlines are important for things like making sure the horizon is level and making sure that walls and other structures are exactly at 90 degrees.

To turn these gridlines on, go to Settings > Camera > Grid and slide the switch to the On position.

Burst Mode

Have you ever attempted to photograph a moving thing with your iPhone? Frequently, the object is long gone by the time your phone processes the photograph. Even if you do manage to get a picture, the subject is often blurry and distorted.

The remedy is to utilize Burst Mode. This requires a quick succession of images that will provide you with a variety of photographs from which to choose. You may retain the finest and reject the others.

Go to Settings > Camera and activate it. Use Volume Up for Burst to enable Burst Mode. Then, keep your finger on the Volume Up button while shooting. Burst Mode will engage immediately and continue until your finger is released.

Enable Live Photo

When attempting to capture the ideal image, you can also utilize Live Photo. Although a Live Photo seems to be a standard image in the Photo Library, when you press and hold it, the captured moment comes to life. Tap the circle icon in the top right corner of the Camera app to turn on Live Photos.

It's a great alternative to burst shots if you don't want dozens of the same pictures in your photos. Your smartphone photography will suffer. Live Photo captures the 1.5 seconds before and after a photograph is taken. Later, you may convert your live photo to a still image.

Benefit from the iPhone Camera Timer

Perhaps one of the least utilized iPhone camera settings is the timer. If you like snapping selfies, this is the ideal device for you. You can utilize a nearby ledge, line up the shot, and still have plenty of time to get into position without having to perform arm gymnastics to include everyone in the frame.

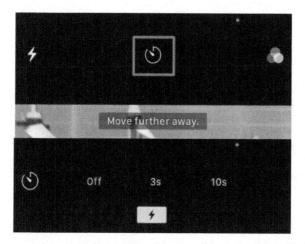

Tap the arrow icon in the bar at the top of the camera window, then tap the Timer icon that appears at the bottom to utilize the timer.

You may choose between a 3- and 10-second timer.

Choose your options and build your image. The timer will not start until the shutter button is pressed.

Mirror Your Front-Facing Camera

Many of us may not realize it, but it takes time and effort to find the angle that shows off our best features in a selfie.

Plus, not everyone is photogenic by nature. Putting on a genuine yet photograph-worthy grin can be difficult.

After all that work, it's annoying to look in the mirror and see your image backward; mirrored selfies are usually not as pretty.

To avoid this, ensure that Mirror Front Camera is on in your iPhone's camera settings. Find advice on how to prevent your iPhone selfies from being mirrored.

Mute the Noise of the Camera

It's not clear why phone makers think people want to hear a fake camera shutter sound every time they take a picture. It is the most irritating thing ever.

Unfortunately, there is no iPhone camera setting that permanently disables noise. You have two options for preventing the sound. To turn the volume off entirely, you may either use the switch on the side of your device or the Volume buttons.

If you choose the latter, you must do it before opening the Camera app, as using the Volume buttons within the app will capture a photo.

Some nations, like Japan and South Korea, prohibit silencing this noise. In certain areas, following these recommendations has no effect.

Enable Geolocation for Your Photographs

Are you a traveler? If so, you may find it helpful to identify your photographs with the place where they were taken. It will help you keep track of all your recollections over the years.

You can turn on geotagging on your iPhone, but it's not clear where to find the setting because it's not in the Camera app or the Camera settings menu. You must instead navigate to the Privacy menu. In Settings > Privacy > Location Services, select While Using App from the Camera menu.

Keep in mind that you may toggle this function on and off at will without altering the location data that your phone has already assigned to previous images.

Live Photo Mode

Technological advancements have been substantial in the previous few decades. The days of disposable cameras, Polaroids, and even point-and-shoot models are all but over; nowadays, the majority of us just pull out our phones and press a button.

If you own an iPhone or iPad, you can also take Live Photos.

When you press and hold your finger on a Live Photo, it "activates" and plays a few seconds of video and audio. They are similar to GIFs with music and are a delightful addition to your photo collection.

However, they are only compatible with Apple devices; if you attempt to play them on any other device, you will only see still images.

For Live Photos, you'll need an iPhone 6s or later, an iPad (5th generation) or later, an iPad Air (3rd generation), an iPad mini (5th generation), or any iPad Pro released in 2016 or later.

How to capture a live image with an iPhone. On the home screen of your iPhone or iPad, launch the Camera application.

Verify that Live Photos are enabled by touching the symbol that resembles a bullseye. It will be located at the top of the screen on the upcoming iPhone. It was shown on screenshots upper.

If the Live Photo symbol is yellow, then the feature is activated. A white space with a black line through it indicates an error. By pressing the symbol, you may enable or disable Live Photo at any moment.

When you press the Live Photos icon on an iPhone 11 or later, you will also be given the "Auto" option. This will allow your iPhone to select whether to shoot a live photo based on the amount of motion it detects.

Using this icon, Live Photos may be instantly toggled on or off. William Antonelli/Insider 3. Aim your phone towards the subject you wish to photograph and press the shutter button as usual. You may also use filters like you would with any other photo.

Your Live Photo will be saved in the camera roll.

Editing a live image on an iPhone or iPad

- You may apply several effects to your live photo.
- Open the Photos app on your device and select the Live Photo you want to change.
- Swipe up while the Live Photo is open to show the Effects menu.

- Under Effects, you have the choice to leave the Live Photo as is or modify it with the following options:
- which will loop the Live Photo video indefinitely.
- Bounce causes your Live Photo to oscillate back and forth.
- Long Exposure, which will combine each Live Photo frame into a single image.

For example, the "Loop" option transforms your Live Photo into a homemade GIF.

William Antonelli/Insider 4. Simply save your effect by quitting the photo; nothing else is required. However, you may modify the impact at any moment by repeating the methods mentioned above.

You may also edit the "Key Photo" — the image that shows when your Live Photo is still — and the video of the Live Photo.

1. Launch the Live Photo and select Edit in the upper-right corner.
2. Toggle the Live Photo icon at the bottom of the page.

A slider will show beside each Live Photo frame. Slide the white window to select a new Key Photo, or use the edge arrows to crop the Live Photo.

You may use the other icons to alter the image's hue, apply a filter, or crop it. William Antonelli/Insider

How to disable live photo capture on an iPhone or iPad

If you want to disable Live Photos — for example, if you want to snap a decent still shot without worrying about the video component — it is simple to do so.

When you open the Camera app, you can turn off Live Photos by touching the symbol and making it look like a slash.

If a slash appears through the Live Photos icon, the feature is deactivated. William Antonelli/Insider

If you wish to permanently disable Live Photos so that they are not automatically activated when you take a photo: When Portrait mode is active, the name of the selected lighting effect, such as Natural Light, turns yellow.

- Launch the Settings application and tap the Camera option.
- Tap Preserve Settings and ensure that the Live Photo setting is activated.

Portrait mode

In portrait mode, the camera provides a shallow depth of focus. This allows you to take In addition to True Tone flash, you can also set duration and apply filters. photographs with the subject in crisp focus and the background blurred.

Take portrait photographs:

- Open the Camera app and select Portrait mode with a swipe.
- Follow the on-screen instructions.
- The Shutter button should be pressed.

The Camera application notifies you whether you are too close, too far away, or if the environment is too dim. When you're done taking a picture, you can use the built-in editing tools to do things like crop and auto-enhance.

Some iPhone models offer numerous settings for Portrait mode, including 1x or 2x. Simply press the 1x or 2x button to toggle between the available settings.

Portrait mode photos on iPhone XR and iPhone SE (2nd generation) require the rear-facing camera to recognize a face.

Portrait mode is available on iPhone SE (2nd generation) and subsequent models, iPhone X, and later models, along with iPhone 7 Plus and iPhone 8 Plus.

Folders for photos

The majority of us have encountered the issue of a disorganized photo collection at some time in our lives. The Images app displays a plethora of screenshots, photos of people, events, and aesthetic graphics, all of which you presumably do not like to lose. Fortunately, the Photos app's categories and albums allow you to organize all of your photos, so you can always locate what you're searching for without having to erase anything.

Below, we will demonstrate how to arrange your photographs using albums and folders.

How to Create a Photos Album

By creating an album in the Photos app on an iPhone or iPad, you may instantly organize images of a certain person or event. How to build an album is as follows:

- Launch the Photos app, then navigate to the Albums tab.
- Click the plus sign (+) in the upper-left corner.

- Choose New Album from the menu dropdown.

- Enter the album's title and hit Save.
- Select all the photographs you wish to include in your album and hit the Done button. You can pick between All Photos and existing Albums.

To add more images to your album, simply open it and click the Add button in the upper-right corner of your screen. Using the symbol with three horizontal dots, you may also Sort and Rename your album. Albums are an excellent way to keep your photographs organized and accessible.

How to Create a Photo Folder

Alternatively, you may create a folder in your Photos application. The distinction between albums and folders is that you cannot add individual photographs to folders, only existing albums and folders. Instead, you may upload images to these albums within the folders.

Create a folder for all of your travels, then create an album for each specific vacation within that folder. You may also convert individual trips into subfolders and create additional albums for certain events, locations, and occurrences throughout the trip.

Let's see how to create a folder in the Photos application:

- Launch Photos and go to Albums.
- Click the plus sign (+) in the upper-left corner.
- Select New Folder.
- After entering the folder's name and pressing Save, the folder will be created.

How to Include an Album in a File

Creating a new album within your new folder involves almost the same fundamental processes, except you must first access the folder. Here's how to proceed:

- Open the folder to which you would like to add a new album or folder.
- Click Edit in the upper-right-hand corner.
- Tap the plus sign (+). Choose New Album or New Folder based on personal desire.

- Add the name, then hit the Save button. You can add images to your new album in the same manner as previously instructed.

People and Places in photos

The Images app looks at your photos to help you quickly find the people, places, and things they contain. The Images app looks at your photos to help you quickly find the people, places, and things they contain.

Depending on how many images you have, you can view a Memory movie of them.

And when iCloud Photos is enabled, the individuals you favorite or name are updated across all of your Apple devices.

Find someone in the album People.

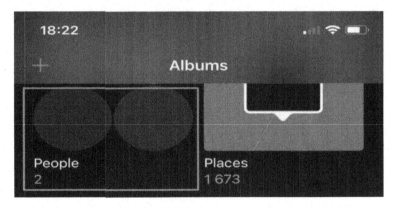

- The Photos application arranges the photographs of people inside the People album.
- For each individual your device detects, a face thumbnail will appear. To locate an individual in your People album:
- Initiate the Photos app.
- Select the Albums tab.
- Listen to People's albums.

- If you've given a person a name in the Photos app, you may also locate them through the Search option. Simply hit Search and then input the individual's name.
- Add an individual to the People album
- Open a photograph of the individual you wish to add.
- Tap the Info button, then the individual's face with a question mark.
- Tap Tag With Name, then enter the individual's name or tap the name if it appears.
- Tap Next, followed by Done.
- Match a face with a name

Photos proposes names from your Contacts, but you may manually add a name to an individual who is already in the People album:

- Launch the People album, then press the person's thumbnail to name them.
- Select Add Name at the top of the display.
- Type the individual's name or choose it if it appears.
- Tap Next, followed by Done.
- Combine images of the same individual.

Occasionally, the same individual is identified in many groups inside your People album. To combine all photographs into one group:

- Select the People album with the Select button.
- Select the individuals you wish to combine.
- Near the bottom of the screen, tap Merge.
- To confirm the merging, tap Yes.
- Incorporate "Feature Less" into the People album.
- With iOS 14 and later, the Photos app might less frequently propose particular individuals. This modifies how the Pictures app curates your Memories, Featured photographs, and the photos displayed in the Photos widget so that you see fewer photos of these individuals. This is how:
- Tap the person's thumbnail in the People album.
- Tap the More link in the upper-right corner of the screen.
- Select "Feature [Name] Fewer."

- Choose an option, such as Feature This Person Less Often or Never Feature This Person, and then press Confirm.

If you want to feature someone less prominently, you will need to reset your Memories settings in order to view that person in the People album again. Go to Settings > Photos, then press Reset Suggested Memories, followed by Reset.

In lieu of reducing a person's rating, you can delete them from the People album. Follow steps 1 and 2, then touch "Remove [name] from People." You may add them whenever you like.

Chapter 4: iPhone Contacts

How to add Contacts

Without your contacts, the iPhone would be incomplete. You can import your contacts from Google or iCloud, but you might need to add a contact to your iPhone by hand sometimes. Here is how it operates.

How to Add a Contact using the Phone App

You may add a new contact using the "Phone" and "Contacts" applications. The procedure is the same. In this example, the Phone app will be utilized (as you might already be familiar with it).

- Open the "Contacts" tab in the "Phone" app on your iPhone.

- Tap the "+" symbol in the upper-right corner of this page.
- You may add the new contact's initial name, last name, and company information from the top
- Tap the "Add Phone" button first after scrolling down.
- This will display a new phone field. Enter their phone number in this field.
- You may now scroll down to enter their email address, address, birthdate, and any further remarks.
- To assign a custom ringtone, navigate to the "Ringtone" menu. You can also enable Emergency Bypass from this

screen to allow their calls through even when Do Not Disturb is engaged.

● Finally, scroll to the top. To add a photo to a contact, click the "Add Photo" option.

On the subsequent screen, numerous profile photo alternatives will be displayed. You have the option of using a photo from your camera roll, a Memoji, or an Animoji.

Tap "Photos" to select a picture from your Camera Roll.

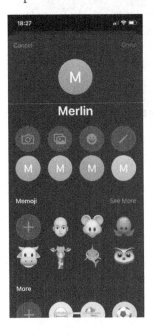

Here, you may view all of your photographs. To choose a picture, tap on it.

Now, you may reposition and resize the image to fit within the circle. Then, click the "Select" button.

Finally, you may apply a filter to your profile photo. To save the profile photo, tap the "Done" button.

You will be returned to your profile photo screen. Tap the "Done" button in the upper-right corner once again.

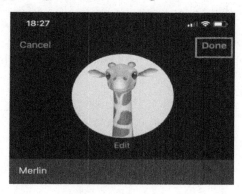

Now, examine the new contact creation page to ensure that everything appears correctly. Tap "Done" to store the contact information.

The contact will now appear in the Contacts app on your iPhone.

Add a Contact to the Call Log

Frequently, if you wish to save the number of the person who just phoned you. In this scenario, the phone number itself is not required.

On your iPhone, launch the "Phone" application and navigate to the "Recents" tab.

Find the number you wish to store and then hit the I button located on the screen's right side.

Tap the "Add New Contact" button now.

You will be presented with the "New Contact" screen (from the above section). The distinction, in this case, is that the phone number has already been inserted. You may now complete the remaining fields, including a profile photo. To save the contact, hit the "Done" button after you are completed it.

How to Locate and Contact a Person

If you are unfamiliar with the iPhone, you may be asking how to locate a stored contact. There is the conventional method, as well as a handful of expedient alternatives.

Open the "Contacts" tab in the "Phone" app on your iPhone. To locate the contact, hit the "Search" bar at the top of the screen.

Choose the contact from the search results to view their information in full.

Now, hit "Call" to initiate a phone call.

You may also utilize Spotlight Search to swiftly locate and call a contact.

On the home screen of your iPhone, scroll down to see the search bar. Simply enter the contact's name here. Their contact page will be at the top of the list. To call someone, use the "Call" icon next to their name.

The quickest method, though, is to use Siri. On iPhones with Face ID, hold down the Side button and speak "Call (contact name)" To activate Siri on earlier iPhones with Touch ID, press and hold the fingerprint sensor.

Siri will ask you which number you wish to dial if this is the first time you've dialed it. Siri will then place the call immediately for you.

Changing Contacts

You may attach a photo to a contact, alter a label, and add a birthday using the Contacts app.

Tap a contact, followed by Edit.

Perform any of the subsequent:

- Affix a picture to a contact: Tap Add an image. You may snap or add a photo from the Photos app.
- Add a pronunciation by selecting Edit, scrolling down and tapping "add field," selecting a pronunciation name field, and then entering how to pronounce your contact's name. Siri will then utilize the specified pronunciation when saying the user's name.
- Replace a label: Hit the label, then choose one from the drop-down menu, or tap Add Custom Label to design your own.
- Add a birthdate, social media profile, and more: Tap alongside the item.
- Permit calls or texts from a contact to override the default setting. Do Not Disturb: Tap Ringtone or Text Tone, and then toggle Emergency Bypass on.

- Add remarks: Tap the Notes section.
- Add a prefix, phonetic name, and more elements: Tap "add field" and then choose an option from the list.
- Delete contact details: Tap alongside a field.
- Tap Done when you're finished.

To modify how your contacts are displayed and arranged, navigate to Settings > Contacts.

Favourites and how to use them

The "Favorites" area of the iPhone's Phone app makes it easy to locate your most essential contacts. Here's how to select which contacts display in this section.

You may also configure Do Not Disturb so that you can always be reached by your preferred contacts, even if other incoming calls do not ring your iPhone. This can be crucial in a crisis.

Since Favorites have been since the earliest days of the iPhone, you have likely forgotten that they exist. And it's a pity because this functionality is quite handy.

Adding a Contact to Favorites

To add a contact to favorites, launch the Phone app (the one with the green phone symbol) and tap "Favorites" before hitting "+" in the upper-left corner.

Next, locate the desired contact and tap on their name.

You will now be presented with all possible entry types for the selected contact. These are "Message", "Call", "Video", and "Mail". Select the type of bookmark you wish to create. This is the action that will be executed when the favorite is pressed to activate it. For this tutorial, let's choose "Message."

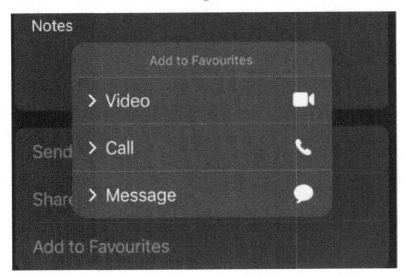

Now, every accessible telephone number or email address will be shown. Tap the item you wish to mark as a favorite.

The process is complete, and you now have a new Favorites entry. Tap it to initiate a chat in Messages, a phone or video call, or a new email, depending on the choices you selected previously.

Black list for Annoying Contacts

Prevent phone calls, FaceTime calls, and messages from specific people.

In the Phone app, you can perform any of the following actions:

Choose from Favorites, Recents, and Voicemail. Hit the contact or number you wish to block, scroll down, and then tap Block this Caller.

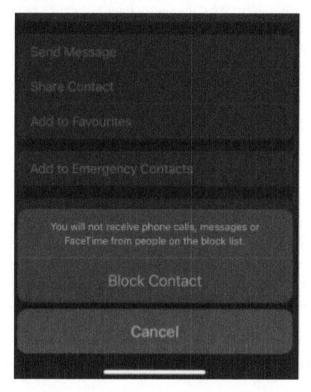

Tap Contacts then hit the contact whose calls you wish to block, scroll down, and then tap Block this Caller.

Chapter 5: Paying via phone

Whether you're shopping at your favorite online retailer or at a brick-and-mortar retailer like Target or McDonald's, paying with your phone is frequently easier and faster than searching for your credit card or exact cash amount. This is why mobile payment applications are gaining popularity among customers.

Apple Pay is the standard payment option for owners of the iPhone, iPad, Apple Watch, and Mac. By linking a credit or debit card via the app, your iPhone or Apple Watch may be used to make in-person and online purchases. Additionally, you may use your iPad or Mac to purchase products from approved websites. When you verify the purchase with Face ID, Touch ID, or a PIN, the funds will be deducted from your account.

Apple Pay requires a suitable device and operating system version(Opens in a new window). For example, you can use the app with iOS 8.1, but you need iOS 15.5 or later to send and receive Apple Cash payments. Here's how you configure Apple Pay on any device you own.

Configuring Apple Pay on an iPhone

Open the Wallet app on your iPhone and hit the plus (+) icon in the upper-right corner, then select Debit or Credit Card and tap Continue. You may now add a credit or debit card in two different methods. You may use the camera on your smartphone to record your name, number, and expiration date.

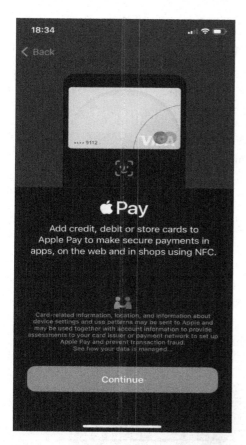

Alternatively, you may enter the number and expiration date manually by tapping Enter Card Details Manually. You must manually input the security code on the back of the card using either method. Then, enter the expiration date and accept the terms and conditions by tapping Next.

Then, you must authenticate your card through email, text message, or phone call to the bank. After entering the code, your card will be authorized and added to the Wallet app for usage with Apple Pay in the future.

If you wish to set up Apple Pay on your iPad in order to make online or in-store purchases, you will discover there is no Wallet app. You must instead add a card via Settings > Wallet & Apple Pay > Add Card.

To add a new card, select Debit or Credit Card, then input the card details as you would on an iPhone. To add a previously added payment method to your iPhone, tap Previous Cards. A list of the cards you've added on your iPhone will appear.

Deselect any you do not wish to add to the iPad, and then touch Continue. Then, you will be required to validate the card through text message, email, or phone call with the card issuer.

Add a Card for Apple Pay

Apple Card, the company's credit card, may also be attached to Apple Pay and shared with family members. Hit the addition (+) icon in the Wallet app, then tap Apply for Apple Card and Continue. Enter your date of birth and address, then confirm your name and phone number.

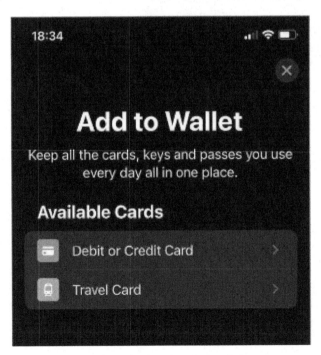

The final four digits of your Social Security number are then required for identification verification. Tap the Next button, then input your annual income. Press Next, review the Apple Card terms and conditions, then tap Agree.

If you are authorized, a screen should display your credit limit, APR, and costs. Tap Accept Apple Card to receive the card. Tap Set as Preferred Card to make Apple Card your preferred payment option for Wallet, Apple Watch, Safari, Apple ID, and Apple Pay.

You also have the option of receiving a real titanium Apple Card for usage at retailers that do not accept Apple Pay. To obtain the card, press Continue, then verify your address and hit Confirm.

The activity screen for your Apple Card should then appear, which will be populated with a balance and activity after you begin using the card.

Customize Apple Pay Configurations

After adding several cards to Apple Pay, there are a number of options that may be modified to enhance the user experience. Navigate to Settings > Wallet & Apple Pay on your iPhone.

You may modify the following from your iPhone:

- Enable or eliminate the requirement to double-click the Side button in order to see your cards.
- Enable or deactivate the usage of Apple Pay in Safari AutoFill on pages that support it.
- Permit your phone to verify payments on neighboring Mac computers.
- Orders may be added immediately to the Wallet app.
- Modifying Your Default Card

On your iPhone, iPad, and Mac, you may alter the default card. This is the card that shows automatically after you pay for an item. To accomplish this, navigate to the Wallet & Apple Pay settings page and hit Default Card under Transaction Defaults. Select the card you would want to use.

Guide to Using Apple Pay

Now that Apple Pay is configured on all of your devices, you may utilize the app. Place your iPhone (or iPad) in close proximity to the terminal or payment scanner if you wish to pay for an item in a brick-and-mortar store using it. Once positioned appropriately, Apple Pay should display your default card.

Swiping up on your card list allows you to select a different card. Tap the option you wish to utilize. When you're ready to pay, double-tap and then press the Side button on your smartphone, and then confirm the transaction using Face ID, Touch ID, or a PIN.

When asked, double-tap the side button on your iPhone or iPad to pay for an online transaction. The payment must then be confirmed using Face ID, Touch ID, or a PIN.

To use your Apple Watch to pay for an item in a physical shop or on a website, double-tap the Side button to show your debit and credit cards. Double-tap the Side button to purchase the item after tapping the desired card.

Visit a website or app that accepts Apple Pay in order to pay for an item online using your Mac. Click the item's pricing or purchase button, then use Touch ID to authenticate the transaction. The item is afterwards bought.

Chapter 6: Using Apps

Opening and closing apps

Even iOS applications can occasionally crash, freeze, or otherwise cease functioning. If you're new to iOS or have never had this problem before, you might not know how to close an app other than by swiping it off the screen. Here's how to close an app and, if necessary, turn off your phone.

Quit an app

- Open the App Switcher by sliding up from the bottom of the screen and pausing in the center, or by double-pressing the Home button (if your device has one).
- You will get an overlapped view of all open applications. Swipe to the right or left until the app you wish to close is located.

- Swipe up to close the application.

- To locate an app, use the App Switcher and swipe to the side.
- When you locate the problematic application, swipe it up to close it.
- There is no method to shut all of your applications simultaneously, but you can close up to three apps at once by using the right number of fingers. Otherwise, if you have many apps active, you will have to swipe them off one by one.

Apps that everyone uses and what are they for

Facebook Messenger

Messenger (12+)
Text, audio and video calls
Meta Platforms, Inc.

#5 in Social Networking
★★★★★ 4.1 · 1.3M Ratings

Free

No matter how you feel about the most popular social network, its messaging software is the best. You don't need a phone number to use Facebook Messenger, and you can use it on any device, unlike WhatsApp, which requires your phone to be present. Unlike iMessage, it operates on all platforms. It also includes a slew of interesting features, such as voice calling and video chatting with AR masks, stickers, and mobile payments. You may even play games with your connections using it. Oh, and it's all free.

Gmail

Gmail - Email by Google (4+)
Secure, fast & organized email
Google LLC

#1 in Productivity
★★★★★ 4.5 · 571.2K Ratings

Free · Offers In-App Purchases

Google's email app is an excellent means of communication. It, like the wonderful Microsoft Outlook, allows you to view mail from Hotmail, Yahoo, and other providers via IMAP. Gmail does not connect your calendar in the same manner as Outlook for iPhone does, but it makes managing your complete email database easier than the preloaded Apple Mail software. It's quick and easy, and it even allows you five seconds to cancel sending.

Kik

Many messaging applications need you to share your phone number with individuals with whom you connect, while Kik simply requires a username. Kik, which has a bot store with over 6,000 bots, beat Facebook Messenger and Skype to the area of artificial conversationalists. This youth-oriented app's appeal is enhanced with group chat, photo and video sharing, and games.

Outlook

Microsoft Outlook

Secure Email, Calendar & Files

Microsoft Corporation

#13 in Productivity

★★★★★ 4.8 • 5M Ratings

Free · Offers In-App Purchases

Microsoft Outlook's lightweight and adaptable mobile email client supports virtually every email account you possess, contains an integrated calendar, and has a Focused inbox that only shows essential messages. The software is often updated, has an auxiliary Apple Watch app, and supports 3D Touch. The Outlook iPhone app, unlike the rest of Office Mobile, is completely free.

Skype

Skype 12+

Talk. Chat. Collaborate.

Skype Communications S.a.r.l

#21 in Social Networking

★★★★★ 4.6 • 62.5K Ratings

Free · Offers In-App Purchases

Skype is one of the top free iPhone communication apps. The software allows video calls and rich messaging with animated emoticons. A good bot selection provides useful information as well as amusement. This iPhone software, like other Skype versions, allows you to call or chat with other Skype users for free, or buy credit to call any other phone number, landline, or mobile. You may even acquire a phone number that allows anyone to call your Skype account from any phone.

Viber

Viber Messenger: Chats & Calls 17+

Message with Confidence

Viber Media SARL.

#24 in Social Networking

★★★★★ 4.6 • 425.3K Ratings

Free · Offers In-App Purchases

The ability to effortlessly move calls from mobile to desktop and vice versa was an early distinction for Viber, a software that allows you to send sticker-emblazoned texts, make calls, engage in video conversations, and make free calls to regular phones. Despite the fact that it requires your phone number, it encrypts communications.

Information and education

ASL App

The ASL App [12+]
Learn ASL Anywhere!
Ink & Salt LLC
Designed for iPad

★ ★ ★ ★ ★ 3.0 • 748 Ratings

Free · Offers In-App Purchases

The ASL Software is a free iPhone app designed exclusively for learning American Sign Language, and it's a good start. It teaches you the alphabet, several useful words and phrases, and the necessary motions through movies. The free edition covers the fundamentals, but in-app purchases offer advanced content in 99-cent packs. For $9.99, you receive access to all of the app's features.

Bing

Microsoft Bing Search [17+]
Private, Fast and Unbiased
Microsoft Corporation

#158 in Utilities
★ ★ ★ ★ ★ 3.7 • 115.6K Ratings

Free

People frequently overlook the fact that there are other ways to locate webpages, instructions, movies, and photographs on the Internet.

There are numerous compelling reasons to consider alternatives to market leader Google, and the Bing app for the iPhone demonstrates some of them. Bing features a beautiful, clean, and easy-to-use interface.

Bing's app keeps up in terms of features, adding voice and camera interaction as well as local information.

Furthermore, rather than simply a blank search bar, the Bing app's home screen provides local assistance and news choices.

Duolingo

Duolingo - Language Lessons 4+
Learn Spanish, French, German
Duolingo

#1 in Education
★★★★★ 4.7 • 1.6M Ratings

Free · Offers In-App Purchases

Could learning a new language provide benefit to individuals all around the world? It's an odd concept, but it's one that comes to life when you use the free language learning program Duolingo.

The Duolingo iPhone app is without a doubt the greatest free language-learning program available. A recent update makes your upcoming courses available offline, allowing you to study even when you are not connected to the Internet.

Flipboard

Flipboard is a digital magazine-style software that curates material from your social networks and online partners (think magazines and blogs) depending on your interests. The software is available for free download and requires a free user account. Flipboard thrives on the iPad, taking use of swiping movements with both aesthetic and interactive beauty, but despite the smaller size, it's still attractive on the iPhone.

NASA

NASA 4+
NASA
★ ★ ★ ★ ★ 4.8 · 62.8K Ratings
Free

NASA has produced several iPhone applications, the most of them have a specialized emphasis (NASA Television, ISSLive, NASA Space Weather). However, this is the space agency's flagship app, and it gathers a wide range of NASA information in that capacity. Space fans and curious minds will appreciate how it condenses a multitude of news items, features, photographs, video, and information on NASA's activities into a single mobile app.

Rosetta Stone

Rosetta Stone: Learn Languages 4+
Speak Spanish, French, German
Rosetta Stone, Ltd.
#35 in Education
★ ★ ★ ★ ★ 4.8 · 184.1K Ratings
Free · Offers In-App Purchases

Rosetta Stone, our top option for advanced language-learning software, has a mobile app that matches the online lectures. When you connect into the mobile app, you may resume your study where you left off. Its streamlined layout is simple to use and allows you to keep up your practice even on the go. It is not inexpensive, but it is the most effective approach to learn a new language.

Wikipedia

Half the joy of owning a smartphone is using it to look stuff up when you're in the thick of a bar bet—and hopefully being correct.

In the mobile age, Wikipedia is the go-to source for fact-checking, and the Wikipedia app typically provides information faster than a mobile search engine.

WolframAlpha

WolframAlpha is similar to Wikipedia, however it focuses on

mathematics and science. It's an excellent source of information and calculation on practically any topic, from elementary algebra to the intricacies of the cosmos. The app, as you might assume, requires an Internet connection to function.

Entertainment

Netflix

Netflix has become a cultural phenomenon, as have many of the other applications listed here. Many consider original, exclusive shows like The Crown, House of Cards, and Stranger Things to be better to much of what is available on broadcast or cable. Add to it a slew of classic standbys from both television and film releases, and you've got yourself a must-have service. Much of the content may now be downloaded for offline viewing. It's worth noting that this is one of the few paid applications on this list, with memberships beginning at $7.99.

Cameo

Cameo - Personal celeb videos 12+
Connect & create with celebs
Baron App, Inc.

#173 in Photo & Video
★★★★★ 4.8 • 19.3K Ratings

Free · Offers In-App Purchases

Celebrities are just like the rest of us! Cameo allows you to pay renowned people of various sizes to record a personalized video greeting. Are you getting married?

Allow an actor to congratulate you. Do you need to motivate a student before a huge exam? Recruit a musician. It's a lot more exciting than waiting in line for an autograph.

Crunchyroll

Crunchyroll 17+
Stream anime shows and movies
Ellation, Inc.

#29 in Entertainment
★★★★★ 4.6 • 504.1K Ratings

Free · Offers In-App Purchases

Crunchyroll is the ad-free streaming service for anime (or live-action Asian TV).

It has tens of thousands of episodes, shows that are broadcast from other countries, and various services that fans want, such as social interaction elements.

We do wish it had a Netflix-style suggestion option, though.

Downcast

Downcast 4+
Podcast player
Jamawkinaw Enterprises LLC

#6 in News
★★★★★ 4.3 • 2.2K Ratings

$2.99 · Offers In-App Purchases

Do you enjoy podcasts? Downcast stands out for its amazing

features, intelligent downloading choices, and user-friendly layout. It's far superior than Apple's default Podcasts app, and it's ideal for anyone who want complete control over their podcast listening experience. Downcast allows you to control not only how frequently the podcast catcher checks for new episodes, but also where it is while it does so, thanks to geo-fencing. "Check for new episodes when I get to work," for example.

ESPN

More than most other applications, ESPN's free app allows you to monitor the game for your favorite teams in more sports swiftly and discreetly (that is, with your phone beneath the dinner table).

Top experts provide scores, headlines, and a live Twitter-like stream. Baseball, basketball, football, soccer, tennis, ice hockey, cricket, racing, rugby, WWE, and other sports are covered.

Hulu

Hulu: Stream shows & movies 12+
Watch films & tv episodes
Hulu, LLC
#6 in Entertainment
★★★★★ 3.C • 1.1M Ratings
Free · Offers In-App Purchases

Hulu is the greatest site for legally watching new and vintage domestic and foreign TV shows shortly after they broadcast, and it also has some good films and a notably large anime collection.

You can even watch live material if you have a Hulu with Live TV subscription.

Pocket Casts

Pocket Casts 9+

Powerful podcast player

Automattic

#58 in News

★★★★★ 3.9 · 2.8K Ratings

Free · Offers In-App Purchases

There are plenty excellent podcasts available for listening on your iPhone. Unfortunately, Apple's podcast app does not do them credit.

Pocket Casts is one of the finest podcast catchers and players on the iPhone, thanks to its excellent podcast discovery and extensive settings and features, including the ability to sync your listening experience across various devices.

LiveOne

LiveOne Music 12+

Slacker, Inc.

Designed for iPad

★★★★★ 4.7 · 25.8K Ratings

Free · Offers In-App Purchases

LiveOne has replaced Slacker Radio. It always seems to pound a few beats faster than the others.

The updated app combines the company's live music and video feeds with Slacker Radio's expert DJs and vast music library to create one of the most comprehensive streaming music services available today.

SoundCloud

SoundCloud: Discover New Music [12+]
Find new trending playlists
SoundCloud Global Limited & Co KG

#4 in Music
★★★★★ 4.5 · 181.6K Ratings

Free · Offers In-App Purchases

SoundCloud has evolved into an audio sensation. The software delivers a beautiful and easy-to-use interface for listening to music.

You can't ignore SoundCloud if you want something else than the popular or if you want to submit your own music. SoundCloud Go eliminates advertisements and allows for unlimited offline track saving for $9.99 per month.

SoundCloud Go+ has a massive catalog of professionally released songs.

Spotify

Spotify - Music and Podcasts [12+]
Discover the latest songs
Spotify

#1 in Music
★★★★★ 4.8 · 23.5M Ratings

Free · Offers In-App Purchases

Spotify has a large archive of music in every genre imaginable, and it even makes playlists based on your listening history. You may now use it to listen to podcasts and music as well as download content for offline listening. Switch between your listening devices with ease from any other device. Listen for free with advertisements, or pay $9.99 a month for ad-free listening as well as other premium features such as 320Kbps high-quality audio.

Twitch

Twitch: Live Game Streaming 17+
Watch Fortnite, PUBG & IRL TV
Twitch Interactive, Inc.

#7 in Photo & Video
★★★★★ 4.? • 1.6M Ratings

Free · Offers In-App Purchases

Twitch's iPhone app does not let you to stream your own gameplay footage, but it is the ideal method to watch your favorite streaming personalities and connect with other gamers on the go.

Twitch is the place to go if you want to watch innumerable individuals, from experts to casual gamers, broadcast any video game you can think of.

It's also mostly free of the stringent copyright restrictions that are now crippling competitor YouTube Gaming. Twitch for iPhone is an excellent portable entry point into the Twitch community.

Vimeo

Vimeo is the mature version of YouTube. Art films and independent projects, as well as animation, sports, music, instruction, and humor, have a higher overall quality level. There will no longer be an overload of kittens, memes, and skateboard wipeout videos.

Not to mention the advertisements and rude remarks on the incumbent internet video service.

Favorite and share videos, follow users who post videos you enjoy, store videos for offline watching, and add videos to your Watch Later queue.

Among the sleek UI elements is a PiP player, which can be used while exploring other aspects of the program.

Finance

Coinbase

Coinbase: Buy Bitcoin & Ether [4+]
Crypto exchange, prices & news
Coinbase, Inc.
Designed for iPhone

#25 in Finance
★★★★★ 4.7 • 1.7M Ratings

Free

Join the Bitcoin frenzy with this feature-rich and well-designed software. You may view current prices and create Bitcoin, Ethereum, and Litecoin digital currency wallets. To safeguard access to your account and create price trigger notifications, you can use Touch ID or Face ID (on the iPhone X).

Groupon

Groupon - Local Deals Near Me [12+]
Activities, Discounts, Coupons
Groupon, Inc.

#56 in Shopping
★★★★★ 4.8 • 417k Ratings

Free

Who can say no to a good deal? Groupon finds local bargains for you, often at steep discounts.

Find deals on products, activities, spas, restaurants, and vacations. Check out what other users thought of the discounts including the super-low "door-buster" prices. You can even use Apple Pay to pay!

Mint

Mint: Budget & Expense Manager ⊞4+
Bill Organizer & Money Saver
Mint.com

#36 in Finance
★★★★★ 4.8 • 753.7K Ratings

Free · Offers In-App Purchases

Mint.com assists you in keeping precise financial records by linking to all of your bank accounts and recording all of the money you make and spend.

The iPhone app provides detailed information on how you spend your money and if you're keeping to your budget. It is one of the greatest personal financial applications available.

Qapital

Qapital: Find Money Happiness ⊞4+
Save. Invest. Share finances.
Qapital, LLC

★★★★★ 4.8 • 80.7K Ratings

Free

Budgeting is serious business, but who says it can't also be a game? iPhone app for personal finance Qapital encourages you to save money through gamification and little daily actions.

It makes saving for future aspirations simple. Simply be prepared to create a new savings account with a modest monthly charge.

Venmo

Venmo [4+]

Send Money, Pay & Earn Rewards

Venmo

#3 in Finance

★ ★ ★ ★ ★ 4.9 • 14.7M Ratings

Free

Devices like Square, as well as built-in services like Apple Pay Cash, make it simple to pay companies without using cash or credit cards. But what if you merely want to repay a pal for a nice night out?

You won't have to scavenge up dollar dollars or remember how to write a check using Venmo. Simply download this app, add your bank account or debit card information, connect with a buddy, and begin letting the money flow.

Venmo also communicates with Facebook, allowing you to share your most bizarre transactions with the rest of the world.

Travel & food

Airbnb

Despite some debate about hotel legislation in some locations, we've had nothing but positive experiences, clean accommodations, and polite hosts through Airbnb. The app contains all of the features you might want and more. Travelers may schedule their stay, interact with the host directly, obtain precise instructions, and experience imaginative lodgings such as equipped tree homes. Through the app, hosts can screen potential boarders, manage their schedules, and market their properties. It's a win-win situation.

GasBuddy

GasBuddy: Find & Pay for Gas [17+]
Cheap fuel prices and rewards
GasBuddy Organization Inc

#31 in Travel

★★★★★ 4.7 • 444.3K Ratings

Free

Yes, driving alone in a combustion-engine car is so passé, but those of us who still use that old 20th-century means of transportation on occasion want to pay as little as possible for gasoline. Gasbuddy displays the cheapest prices at nearby gas stations. I realized that I could either pay $3.19 per gallon in Manhattan or $2.37 in New Jersey. With a large enough tank, that could pay for the tunnel!

Google Maps

Google Maps [4+]
Places, Navigation & Traffic
Google LLC

#1 in Navigation

★★★★★ 4.7 • 4.9M Ratings

Free

Google Maps, another major force on the internet, may contain the most up-to-date and detailed geographic information of any business. It provides excellent turn-by-turn directions by auto, foot, and public transit. The software connects to your Google account to compute travel times based on your home and work addresses. Offline maps, street view, and indoor maps are all useful features. However, after a rocky start, the iPhone's built-in Apple Maps now matches most of its qualities, and rival Here WeGo provides another viable choice if privacy is an issue.

Grubhub

Grubhub: Food Delivery [4+]
Restaurants, Grocery, Alcohol
GrubHub.com

#13 in Food & Drink
★★★★★ 4.7 • 3.7M Ratings

Free

Most cities have lots of delicacies to offer, but accessing them might be difficult. If you reside in or visit any of GrubHub's 1,100+ covered communities in the United States (or London), you can get delicious local cuisine delivered right to your door using the GrubHub iPhone app. Following its merger with competitor Seamless, the service currently serves over 45,000 takeaway establishments. We enjoy how it calls you to let you know when your meal will come, allows you to tip inside the app, and allows you to advise eateries to preserve the planet and avoid using plastic utensils.

Maps.Me

When traveling to remote locations, you may not always be able to connect your iPhone to a data connection, but you still need to know where you are. There's the Maps.Me offline map app for those occasions. It allows you to download a whole city's or country's map data with a single click, so you won't get lost if you don't have mobile or Wi-Fi connectivity. The app displays nearby transit and food options, as well as cycling routes. Because it is based on the open-source OpenStreetMap projects, it does not record your every step while you use it. For $3.49 a year, you can remove the small, unobtrusive ads that fund the project.

OpenTable

OpenTable has long been a popular tool for booking dinner reservations without picking up the phone, and the iPhone app now offers a slew of additional capabilities thanks to TouchID compatibility. You may use Apple Pay to not only make a restaurant reservation, but also to pay for your meal at the end. The revamped interface also takes use of the Plus iPhones' extra-large dimensions.

Paprika Recipe Manager

Paprika Recipe Manager 3 17+

Organize your recipes

Hindsight Labs LLC

#1 in Food & Drink

★★★★★ 4.9 • 34.6K Ratings

$4.99

Paprika is one of our favorite meal planning apps because it may help you become a far more efficient cook. You may store and alter recipes on the web, obtain useful cooking instructions when offline, and upload your own unique recipes using the app.

When planning meals, use grocery lists and the pantry system to keep track of your ingredients. Even better, Paprika is a one-time purchase that does not require a subscription.

Weather Underground

Weather Underground: Local Map 4+
Radar & severe storm tracker
Weather Underground, LLC
Designed for iPad

#15 in Weather
★★★★★ 4.0 • 26.3K Ratings

Free · Offers In-App Purchases

None of us will be able to control the weather like Sean Connery in The Avengers in 1998, or Thor in the other Avengers.

Instead, we rely on weather applications, such as The Weather Channel's, to keep us informed of the weather's vagaries.

This well-designed iPhone software delivers all of the weather information you want, and it even works with Apple Watch.

The Weather Channel

Weather - The Weather Channel 4+
Local Radar Maps & Storm Watch
The Weather Channel Interactive
Designed for iPad

#1 in Weather
★★★★★ 4.7 • 3.4M Ratings

Free · Offers In-App Purchases

Although iOS includes a Weather app, you should avoid it since Weather Underground is considerably superior. It succeeds by sticking to what it does best: plainly providing a large amount of hyper-local information in a simple and highly customisable interface.

This superb app's abundant data will satisfy even the most information-hungry meteorology nerd.

Yelp

Yelp: Food, Delivery & Reviews [12+]
Find great local businesses!
Yelp

#9 in Food & Drink
★★★★★ 4.2 • 692.2K Ratings

Free

Yelp, the most thorough business-reviewing app, turns out to be an excellent tool for locating nearby restaurants, businesses, and services, especially when you're in a location you're unfamiliar with.

You may also take photographs and offer reviews to assist other foodies find a wonderful spot.

Fitness & health

Adidas Training by Runtastic

This software is for anybody who wishes to keep track of their activities, such as cycling, hiking, skiing, kayaking, or simply strolling. It generates a variety of data on your activities and journey.

Your map route, for example, has mile markers, and you can access comprehensive charts to examine your speed, pace, elevation, and other information on each leg. When you use the app while wearing a compatible heart-rate monitor, Runtastic displays that data in your final outputs.

This is one of the greatest running (and sports activity-tracking) applications because of the audio feedback and music integration.

Cyclemeter

Bike Computer - Cyclemeter [4+]
Cycling Tracker GPS
Abvio Inc.

★★★★★ 4.7 • 8.1K Ratings

Free · Offers In-App Purchases

Cyclemeter captures a variety of data, is extremely precise, and has a number of well-thought-out features. Cyclemeter is free to download, but to unlock all of its features, you must spend $9.99 for the Elite in-app purchase.

It tracks and records your bike rides before compiling all of your data into beautiful graphs.

Cyclemeter, despite its name, does more than only record cycling. Other activities, such as cross-country skiing and jogging, are also preloaded.

You can now control several of the fitness app's capabilities with an Apple Watch and save your workout data to iCloud.

Headspace

There's more to fitness than sweating and puffing on the running track. Stress reduction is high on the list, and meditation can help with that.

Headspace has hundreds of guided meditations that might help with anxiety and mindfulness. In-app subscriptions for additional courses begin at $12.99—still a lot less than a shrink!

MyFitnessPal

MyFitnessPal: Calorie Counter [17+]
Macro, Diet & Food Tracker
MyFitnessPal, Inc.

#11 in Health & Fitness
★★★★★ 4.7 • 1.5M Ratings

Free · Offers In-App Purchases

MyFitnessPal, a free health app, is one of the finest all-in-one calorie counter and exercise trackers for the iPhone.

The app's basic design and layout make using it a brief task rather than a time-consuming project, which is critical when trying to achieve a long-term fitness or weight goal.

This app's selling point is its extensive food and nutrition database, which outperforms any competitor's we've seen. A $9.99-per-month in-app membership is required for ad-free access and certain additional functionality.

WebMD

WebMD: Symptom Checker [17+]
Med Reminders, Allergy Alerts
WebMD

#162 in Medical
★★★★★ 4.7 • 108K Ratings

Free

WebMD is much more than a diagnosis app, but you can certainly use it to enter symptoms and uncover some hints as to what's wrong with you.

It also includes listings for nearby healthcare specialists and pharmacies, as well as first-aid guides—basic guidelines for dealing with situations.

This free reference software is one you hope you never need, but when you do, you'll be pleased you did.

Zocdoc

Zocdoc [12+]
Healthcare, but easy
Zocdoc Inc
Designed for iPad

#24 in Medical
★ ★ ★ ★ ★ 4.8 • 10.8K Ratings

Free

If you haven't been diligent about staying in shape with any of the applications mentioned above, have been in an accident or sickness, or are just considering a butt-lift, ZocDoc can connect you with the correct doctor.

It not only finds you a suitable doctor or specialist, but it also makes appointments easy and allows you to view other users' reviews of the physicians you're considering.

The app knows which physicians accept your insurance, suggests different sorts of checkups, and maintains track of your medical visits even if you didn't schedule them through ZocDoc.

Lifestyle & passion

5miles

Before the Internet, if you wanted to buy a used item or a peculiar service that wasn't available in a local business, you crossed your fingers and hoped it was in the classified advertising of your local newspaper. 5 Miles allows you to do so from your smartphone. It's a fantastic, though occasionally shady, digital marketplace that, in its card-like appearance, is similar to Pinterest.

Kickstarter

Kickstarter [12+]
Bring Creativity to Life
Kickstarter, PBC

★★★★★ 4.8 • 45.6K Ratings

Free

With this free entrance, the king of crowdsourcing provides an iPhone software fit for royalty. The Kickstarter app has everything you need, whether you're a backer or a creative. It does not, however, allow you to join up as a creator, which you must still do on the web on a computer. But be careful not to become too engrossed in its appealing UI that you blow your crowdfunding money.

LibriVox

LibriVox Audio Books [4+]
50,000 unlimited audiobooks
BookDesign LLC
Designed for iPad

#54 in Books
★★★★★ 4.8 • 24.9K Ratings

Free · Offers In-App Purchases

LibriVox is a volunteer effort that records audiobooks in the public domain. It's an excellent method to read Dickens or Twain while resting your eyes. You have the option of streaming or downloading. Browse by author or genre, or simply type in what you wish to hear. You may even program a sleep timer if you miss being read to sleep as a youngster. The short audio commercials are removed in the $1.99 Pro edition.

Video & photo editors

Photoshop

Photoshop Express Photo Editor ⁴⁺
Retouch, Collage & Customize
Adobe Inc.

#13 in Photo & Video
★★★★★ 4.8 · 666.9K Ratings

Free · Offers In-App Purchases

Adobe is well-known for producing high-quality photography software, and Photoshop Express is no exception. Excellent lighting and color correction options are available in a simple interface. There are not just elegant preset effect filters, but you can also make your own bespoke ones. The main disadvantage is that certain functions need an Adobe account or in-app payments.

iMovie

Apple's mobile video-editing program is ideal for making your holiday photographs and films watchable—and pleasurable.

iMovie makes it simple to manipulate your footage, including freeze-frame, filters, titles, cutting, and adding background music. And it's now free.

CapCut

CapCut - Video Editor [12+]
Video maker with music
Bytedance Pte. Ltd

#4 in Photo & Video
★★★★★ 4.5 · 171 Ratings

Free · Offers In-App Purchases

CapCut, a simple but surprisingly powerful mobile video editor from the designers of TikTok, is now available. Using the easy touch interface, you may import and rearrange films and photographs.

Furthermore, the stock asset collection and predefined designs make it simple to transform your raw resources into something destined to go viral.

Facetune

Facetune Editor by Lightricks
Photo & Video Editing
Lightricks Ltd.

#11 in Photo & Video
★★★★★ 4.6 · 221.8K Ratings

Free · Offers In-App Purchases

Do you want to improve the appearance of someone's face in an iPhone photo?

Facetune provides a plethora of options to help you accomplish this. This amazing software may help you get smoother skin, healthier hair, brighter grins, and even a more prominent jawline.

Flickr

Flickr not only offers one of the greatest groups of devoted photographers, but its iPhone app has a plethora of picture editing and effect capabilities. The app is excellent at displaying reactions to your images as well as a stream of photos from accounts you follow.

PicsArt

Picsart Photo Editor & Filters [12+]
Video & Image Editing, Effects
PicsArt, Inc.
Designed for iPad

#6 in Photo & Video
★ ★ ★ ★ ★ 4.7 • 910k Ratings

Free · Offers In-App Purchases

PicsArt may be the most imaging-tool-packed program of all time, and it even has its own social network. Overlays, layers, clone stamps, curves, and masks are all available. And, despite the fact that there are so many features, the UI is still crowded in certain places, compared to previous editions.

Prisma

Prisma, which takes mundane smartphone photographs and utilizes AI to make incredibly stunning effects, made quite a stir on the Internet this year.

Make that street scene appear like a Van Gogh painting or that picture look like a Picasso painting. Really!

You have to see this software in action to believe it. It works on its servers rather than locally, so you may have to wait.

ProCamera

ProCamera. 4+
Professional RAW Photo Camera
Cocologics

#31 in Photo & Video
★★★★★ 4.7 • 5K Ratings

$16.99 · Offers In-App Purchases

Whereas most iPhone photography applications are focused with what you do after you've taken a photo, ProCamera is more concerned with the shooting process itself. The software displays an interface similar to that of a digital SLR camera. The ISO, EV (exposure value), shutter speed, and white balance may all be adjusted. Before taking a shot, a stabilizing option waits for the phone to be still. Brilliant.

Productivity

Any.do

Any.do: To do list & Calendar 4+
Planner, Reminders & Tasks
Any.DO
Designed for iPad

★★★★★ 4.6 • 43.6K Ratings

Free · Offers In-App Purchases

Any.do features a feature called the Any.do Moment that encourages you to assess your daily chores.

Geolocation reminders actually function with this app, and it's an excellent software for keeping track of activities and objectives in general.

Asana

Asana: Work in one place [4+]
Get to your goals faster

Asana, Inc.

#114 in Business

★★★★★ 4.7 • 12.4K Ratings

Free

The iPhone version for PCMag's favorite collaboration tool is likewise excellent.

Asana not only displays your tasks and tells you when their status changes, but it also allows you to create new tasks, projects, and kanban boards.

You may contribute comments, files, and photographs from your iPhone, and you can do so while disconnected for later synchronization.

Evernote

Evernote - Notes Organizer [4+]
Note pad, to-do list, planner

Evernote Corporation

#189 in Productivity

★★★★★ 4.4 • 43.3K Ratings

Free · Offers In-App Purchases

The Evernote iPhone app allows you to take notes on the fly and search for information in your account at any time, from any location.

While Evernote has long been a pioneer in the note-taking and syncing field, current plans restrict access to the finest features to the highest-paying customers exclusively.

IFTTT

IFTTT - automation & workflow [4+]

For apps, devices & smart home

IFTTT

★★★★★ 4.8 · 54.1K Ratings

Free · Offers In-App Purchases

If this, then that—shorten that to IFTTT, and you have one of the finest applications on the market. This incredibly simple yet powerful iPhone software can automate almost anything in your digital life.

For example, if I create a new contact in Gmail, I may store that contact's information to my Evernote account.

If you're making your house smart, you should keep the IFTTT app on your iPhone since it can help you control a variety of gadgets, such as shutting off the lights when you get into your smart bed.

Microsoft Office

You definitely don't want to create that report or amend that spreadsheet on your smartphone, but you'd be shocked at how easy Microsoft Office Mobile makes it. Your papers are saved to and synchronized with the versions on OneDrive, allowing you to transition from one form factor to another with ease. For on-the-go productivity, you may download Word, Excel, and PowerPoint. A monthly Office 365 subscription beginning at $6.99 is required.

Todoist

Todoist: To-Do List & Planner [4+]
To do, task reminders & habit
Doist Inc.

#155 in Productivity
★★★★★ 4.8 · 87.4K Ratings

Free · Offers In-App Purchases

Todoist allows you to nerd out on task organization and supports a wide range of platforms and connectors. The commercial edition includes task labels and reminders, location-based reminders, the option to make notes and upload files, and a one-of-a-kind productivity chart.

Social media networking

Cloze

Cloze Relationship Management [4+]
Smart CRM, Inbox and Contacts
Cloze
Designed for iPad

★★★★★ 4.6 · 2K Ratings

Free · Offers In-App Purchases

Cloze is an iPhone software that collects tweets, emails, Facebook posts, and other forms of communication from your contacts and ranks them depending on who is most important to you.

In other words, even if your boss isn't at the top of your Twitter feed chronologically, she will be at the top of your Cloze view. It's a fantastic tool for learning about individuals in your network, and its Web app offers even more features and insights to enjoy.

Instagram

Instagram has eclipsed Flickr as the most popular picture sharing site on the Internet, despite – or maybe because of – its limits. Its social discovery features are addicting, it has outstanding image-editing capabilities, and it now enables video in addition to still photographs. The firm is constantly introducing new features, including as direct messaging, Snapchat-like Stories, and, most recently, pinch-to-zoom. To stay up with the times, the app now supports Handoff for switching between your Apple Watch and iPhone.

Kippo

If poorly handled, a gamer-focused dating app seems like an awful nightmare. Fortunately, Kippo's ingenious design and features make it a friendly refuge for nerds looking for love. You may personalize your beautiful profile to reflect your geeky hobbies, and you can enjoy premium features at a low cost. You may even socialize and play games in a social "metaverse" realm.

LinkedIn

LinkedIn: Network & Job Finder 12+
Connect, Apply & Get Hired
LinkedIn Corporation

#5 in Business
★★★★★ 4.2 • 71.9K Ratings

Free · Offers In-App Purchases

LinkedIn is a useful online network for staying in touch with your contacts. For discovering otherwise long-lost colleagues and business partners, it's natural to rely on LinkedIn more than your own address book.

Anyone in the job market will want to keep up with LinkedIn because of its networking features as well as its fantastic database of job postings. It works great on an iPhone, but the full-sized LinkedIn iPad app performs much better.

Match

Match: Dating & Relationships 17+
Chat, Date, Meet & Find Love
Match Group, LLC

#54 in Social Networking
★★★★★ 3.8 • 115.1k Ratings

Free · Offers In-App Purchases

Match's strong dating service prioritizes long-term partnerships above flings. Match has a clean and contemporary mobile app, even with its slightly older userbase.

On the move, you may browse extensive profiles, establish

discussions, and start video chats. It may be costly, but love is priceless.

Pinterest

Pinterest 12+
Home, fashion, lifestyle ideas
Pinterest
#1 in Lifestyle
★ ★ ★ ★ ★ 4.8 · 4.3M Ratings
Free

Pinterest is a virtual pinboard, but don't let that deceive you. It's for shopping, including virtual window shopping.

Pinterest allows you to organize and share any photographs you find online or in your life. With Pinterest on your iPhone, it's simple to take images outside and publish them to your boards.

You can see what others are pinning on Pinterest, and you can frequently buy the things by following a link to the retailer's website.

Tinder

Tinder - Dating New People 17+
Chat, Date & Meet Friends
Tinder Inc.
#2 in Lifestyle
★ ★ ★ ★ ★ 3.8 · 399.7K Ratings
Free · Offers In-App Purchases

Tinder sparked a dating app revolution that is still being felt today. Tinder is no longer only for desperate people with little social skills; with a rapid, brutally efficient, and widely replicated "hot or not" swiping interface well designed for touch screens, Tinder invites everyone and everyone to hunt for hookups (or more).

Now is the time to find the ideal individual.

Tumblr

Tumblr – Fandom, Art, Chaos 17+
Welcome back to weird.
Tumblr, Inc.

#57 in Social Networking
★★★★★ 4.1 • 300.6K Ratings

Free · Offers In-App Purchases

Tumblr, which is less limited than today's main photo-sharing program, Instagram, extends beyond images, allowing you to submit blog entries, GIFs, videos, and other media. However, reposting is more crucial than posting since it encourages a lot more user involvement. Through its nature of reblogging rather than commenting, the service avoids the bad trolling of other social networks.

Twitter

Twitter 17+
Let's talk.
Twitter, Inc.

#1 in News
★★★★★ 4.6 • 6.5M Ratings

Free · Offers In-App Purchases

Twitter Inc., the business that controls the 280-character social network, did not create its own app for a long time. However, plenty of third parties did, although not all of the resulting apps were worth using. As a result, when Twitter published its official Twitter app—which functioned brilliantly and loaded quickly!—users eagerly incorporated the new tool into their iPhones. It's a no-brainer to have this app if you tweet. If you don't twitter and have been debating whether to join the crowds, the iPhone app makes it simple and handy to do so.

Vero

VERO - True Social [17+]

Social without Ads

Vero Labs Inc

★ ★ ★ ★ ★ 4.1 • 1.2K Ratings

Free

In a world dominated by Facebook, Instagram, and Twitter, it takes a lot for a new social media network to stand out, but Vero could be the one that motivates you to change ship. The program allows users to connect via common interests in movies, photography, and other types of art. Plus, because there are no commercials, algorithms, or data tracking, you are free to simply live.

Part 2: Macbook for Seniors

112

Chapter 1: How to Set Up your MacBook

MacBook Overview

Apple's MacBook is a family of Macintosh-based laptop computers. The MacBook series includes the MacBook (2006-present), the MacBook Pro (2006-present), and the MacBook Air (2008-present). As Apple shifted to using Intel instead of PowerPC processors, the PowerBook and iBook product lines merged to form the MacBook portfolio.

MacBook

From late 2011 through 2014, the manufacture of the original MacBook ended, but it was reintroduced at the start of 2015. The 2015 model, known by titles such as "New MacBook" and "MacBook Retina", had several essential improvements. The Force Touch trackpad and a butterfly mechanism for the keyboard's switches were two advances.

Apple MacBook Pro

The MacBook Pro, sometimes known as the MBP, is a somewhat thicker and potentially more significant notebook than the MacBook. It is designed for customers that require their laptop to handle more heavy jobs, such as video editing, because of its more robust internals. The MacBook Pro was the first Apple notebook to include Apple's proprietary Thunderbolt connector in 2011.

Macintosh Air

The MacBook Air was marketed as a more affordable and portable alternative to the MacBook. Therefore, the MacBook Air is the only model without a Retina Display option. When it debuted in January 2008, the MacBook Air was the smallest and lightest member of the MacBook family.

Using the Trackpad and Keyboard

Mac users lack the ability to handle several computers with a single keyboard and mouse, unlike Windows PC users. Universal Control enables users of macOS and iPadOS to share the same cursor, mouse, trackpad, and keyboard across a Mac and an iPad. Additionally, if you have many Macs or iPads, you may share these controls across them.

Universal Control is presently labeled as a beta feature by Apple, although it appears stable enough to use without issue. This capability is distinct from Sidecar, which allows you to utilize an iPad as a second monitor at home. Only Universal Control permits the independent usage of various devices with the same input modalities.

Universal Control Compatibility

Your devices must satisfy specific prerequisites for this to operate. Your iPad must run iPadOS 15.4 or later, and your Mac must have macOS Monterey 12.0 or later. Additionally, your device must be one of the following:

- MacBook Pro debuted later than in 2016
- Apple MacBook Air models released in 2018 or later
- Mac mini debuted later than 2018
- iMac launched in 2017 or after, in addition to iMac (Retina 5K, 27-inch, Late 2015)
- iMac Pro was released in 2017.
- Mac Pro introduced later than 2019

Using two-factor authentication, you must sign in to each device with the same Apple ID and password. With Bluetooth, Wi-Fi, and Handoff enabled, each device must be within 30 feet of the other. For this to operate, your Mac or cellular-enabled iPad cannot be sharing its internet connection. Now, let's see how everything plays out.

Use Login Screen and Touch ID on Mac

Numerous individuals view passwords as inadequate for security. The first step is to recall them. The only method to guarantee that you will not forget or lose your password is to write it down and keep the paper (or another medium) secure.

If you have a modern MacBook Pro or MacBook Air that supports Touch ID, there is a better method. Instead of a password, Touch ID allows you to use your fingerprint. Touch ID will unlock your Mac, but it is also secure enough to provide access to Apple Pay and other Apple services involving money.

Touch ID is not a complete replacement for passwords. After restarting your Mac, you will need to enter your password. After entering your password to log in, you may utilize Touch ID.

To utilize Touch ID, you must set it up (often a one-time operation) and be ready to use it whenever you like.

How to configure Touch ID

1. Setting up Touch ID on your Mac is a straightforward, one-time operation that requires only a few steps.
2. Dry your hands after washing them. Wet hands are incompatible with Touch ID.
3. Select AppleSystem Preferences from the menu. Displays the System Preferences window.

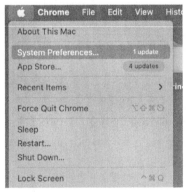

4. Tap Touch ID in the System Preferences window.

5. To add a fingerprint, click +. You are prompted for your password.

6. Provide your password.
7. Select the Touch ID capabilities you wish to employ on your MacBook. Your selections are:
8. Activating your Mac
9. Paying using Apple Pay on iTunes and the App Store
10. Follow the procedures for fingerprint registration.

You must gently press your finger on the Touch ID button and hold it there until registration is complete and you are directed to use another finger. You must register several fingerprints to finish the procedure.

Desktop Settings

Due to Apple's security safeguards, it is impossible to customize your Mac with extensive system modifications. However, there are further methods to personalize your macOS desktop.

Therefore, let's examine how to personalize your Mac desktop in seven simple actions.

1. Begin With a Fresh Wallpaper

Simply replacing the default wallpaper with one of your choosing will revitalize your desktop. To make this little adjustment, launch System Preferences and choose Desktop & Screen Saver.

Choose a new picture from the default Mac desktop themes under the Desktop menu, or opt for a solid backdrop color. In addition, don't forget to check out the Dynamic Desktop area, which features wallpapers that vary according to the time of day.

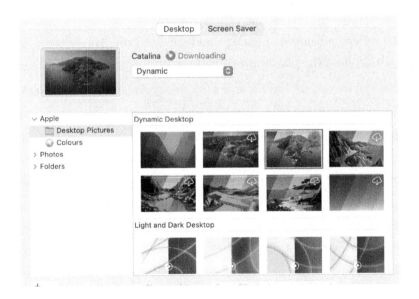

You may also browse your Photos library from the sidebar to set your background to an image you enjoy and don't mind seeing daily. To view different wallpapers from an album, check the Change picture box and select a time interval, such as Every 5 minutes.

2. Create a Unique Color Scheme

Your Mac enables you to mix and match several color settings for system accents and highlights to create your own color scheme. To do so, navigate to System Preferences > General and select new accents and highlight colors.

The altered color scheme will then be mirrored across buttons, boxes, menus, and other system elements.

Alternately, under the same preferences box as above, there is an option to switch to Dark Mode (just after the light one). It is available on all Macs running macOS Mojave or later and provides the Dock, menu bar, program windows, and sidebars with a sleek, black design.

Since you cannot apply system-wide themes to your Mac, you should enable app-specific themes instead. For instance, if you use Alfred to operate your Mac and have enabled the Powerpack, you may modify Alfred's appearance using a custom theme, as outlined on the Alfred Support website.

3. Include Personality-Rich Icons and Backgrounds

In Finder, you can not only resize icons (Select View > Show View Options > Icon size from the menu) but also alter their appearance using custom icons.

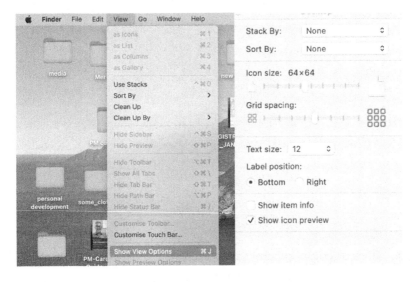

When searching for icons in online repositories, don't forget to look for the ICNS extension (which ensures compatibility with macOS). PNGs and JPGs can also function as icon sources, however, ICNS images that are compatible with macOS are preferable.

To change the icon of a folder (or a file), you must first copy the new icon file (select it and press Cmd + C). Select the folder whose icon you wish to alter, then navigate to File > Get Info.

Select the icon at the top of the inspector window and select Edit > Paste or press Cmd + V. Your personalized icon should now be present. Select it in the inspector and press the Delete key to revert to the default icon if you're not satisfied.

You may even utilize an existing icon as the image source by copying it from the corresponding inspector. Here's a screenshot of the icon for the Music library folder, which has the Apple Music app icon.

Want to replace the default application icons in the Applications folder with your own? Except for the applications that come pre-installed on your Mac, you may do so for everything. However, utilizing the icons of system programs as sources for third-party apps poses no difficulty. You may, for instance, replace the symbol for your preferred third-party web browser with the system icon for Safari.

4. Redesign the Login Page

To customize the login screen on your Mac, begin by changing your account's user image. This is possible via System Preferences > Users & Groups. Select your user account and ensure that the Password tab is selected.

Click the existing user image next to your username to replace it with one from Apple's default collection or your Photos library. Even a Memoji or an Animoji can be substituted. To put the selected image, click Save. Next, you should consider creating an amusing lock screen message. To do so, navigate to System Preferences > Security & Privacy > General and choose the Show a notification when the screen is locked checkbox.

If the option is unavailable, you must click the Lock symbol at the bottom of the pane and enter the system password when requested. Then, you should be able to begin altering it.

Next, select the Set Lock Message option, enter the desired message for the lock screen, and click OK. When you restart your Mac, the notification will appear just above the power options at the bottom of the screen.

5. Get a Better-Looking Dock

To customize the Dock on your Mac, you should at the very least clear it. Remove the icons of seldom-used applications by dragging them out and releasing them when the Remove icon appears. Then, drag your preferred applications from the Applications folder to the Dock.

While hovering, you may also rotate the Dock, resize its icons, and alter their magnification to varying degrees. To access these changes, navigate to System Preferences > Dock & Menu Bar. Alternately, use the following Terminal commands to personalize Dock.

In addition, rather than tinkering with the Dock, you might replace it with a third-party customization option such as uBar.

6. Redesign Individual Applications

To add additional personal touches to your Mac, experiment with the default settings of installed applications. If you have the Slack desktop software installed, for instance, you may customize the Slack sidebar with a new layout.

Change the appearance of your emails in the Mac Mail application

by adjusting the fonts and colors by navigating to Preferences > Fonts & Colors. In addition, you may highlight certain messages by choosing them and selecting a different color from Format > Show Colors.

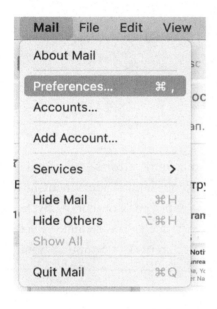

Additionally, you may obtain fresh skin for the Terminal via Preferences > Profiles when it is open. Select one of the available themes in the sidebar and click Default to make it the default. The terminal must be restarted for the new color profile to take effect.

If you're a fan of dark mode, why not enable it in your favorite Mac applications? Numerous applications, including Ulysses, Bear, Things, Tweetbot, and Spark, enable darker themes.

7. Add Custom Sound Effects to Mac

You need not restrict your customization efforts to cosmetic modifications. How about adding some audio adjustments? In System Preferences > Accessibility > Spoken Content > System Voice, you can select a different system voice as the default. Select a new notification sound from System Preferences > Sound > Sound Effects.

In System Preferences > Date & Time > Clock, you may configure your Mac to announce the time at predetermined intervals.

As you can see, with little thought, work, and effort, you can genuinely personalize your Mac. After doing so, it will be much more pleasing to look at and work with. After making all of Instead of those cosmetic adjustments, why not focus on making your Mac more user-friendly for everyday tasks?

How to work with File and Folders

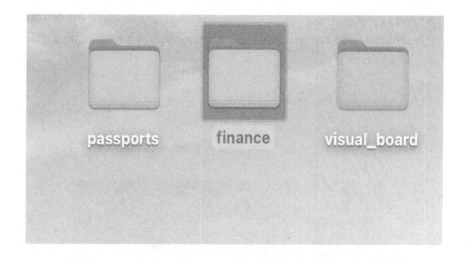

Photos, text documents, and video clips may be stored quickly and easily on a brand-new Mac desktop. As the number of files accumulates, searching for files may become more time-consuming over time. Folders are the answer. Similar to a traditional paper folder, relevant files can be gathered and saved in a single location. In addition, files within a folder can be organized based on certain criteria. Learn how to quickly create, rename, and modify folders on your Mac.

Creating a new folder on macOS is more than a simple procedure.

Every Mac includes pre-installed folders for file management. Included are the Applications, Documents, and Downloads folders in the macOS "Finder" file manager. When you download new fonts for your Mac from the web, for instance, the files are immediately saved in the Downloads folder. On macOS, there are also hidden folders containing crucial system files. If you wish to arrange your data by creating folders on your iMac or MacBook, you have numerous alternatives. Examine all three to see which one best matches your own workflow.

Create a folder on a Mac: option 1

- Go to your Mac's desktop.
- Tap the trackpad with two fingers close together on a MacBook.

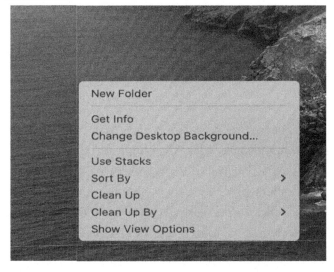

- Once the menu displays, click the "New Folder" option. In a few seconds, the new folder should be added to the desktop.

Create a folder on a Mac: option 2

- Go to your Mac's desktop.

- Enter the following keystroke sequence on your keyboard: ⌘ + Shift + N
- The new folder will appear on your desktop in a few seconds.

Before you can organize your files into folders based on certain criteria, you must rename the newly created folder. This may be accomplished by double-clicking the new folder. The title will be emphasized, and its appearance can be altered as desired. Alternatively, you may just right-click on the folder to bring up a menu on your desktop. To make changes, pick the "Rename" option. You are permitted to alter the name of your folder whenever necessary. Simply drag the relevant files into the corresponding folder to add them to your folder. To accomplish this, hold down the left mouse button until the folder is highlighted in blue. Additionally, you may drag the files into the folder window. Using the choices shown above, you may create subfolders within your folder.To rename the folder you need to tap the touchpad with two fingers at once . Then simply choose the "rename"button.

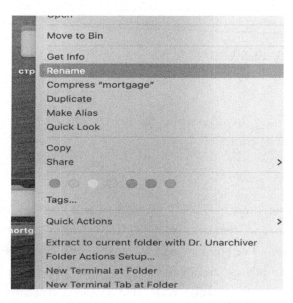

<u>In each folder, any number of subfolders can be created.</u>

Delete folders or individual files by dragging and dropping them into the trash bin in the lower-right corner of the Dock bar. You may alternatively right-click the folder or file to bring up a menu, then pick "Move to Trash" from the menu. If you have accidentally erased a folder, you can also recover your Mac data.

Menu Bar

MacOS is supposed to be user-friendly for the ordinary computer user, yet locating some tools and functions can be difficult, especially when using System Preferences. Fortunately, Mac's menu bar (the thin strip at the top of the screen) has extremely handy shortcuts to the most essential functionalities.

<u>What's on the menu bar on Mac?</u>

The easiest way to utilize the menu bar on a Mac is to become familiar with its contents.

- **Apple menu** - This is where you will find important system tools and features, such as information about your Mac, System Preferences, access to the App Store (and whether app updates are available), recently opened items, and a shortcut for putting your Mac to sleep, restarting your Mac, shutting down your Mac, and logging out of your account.

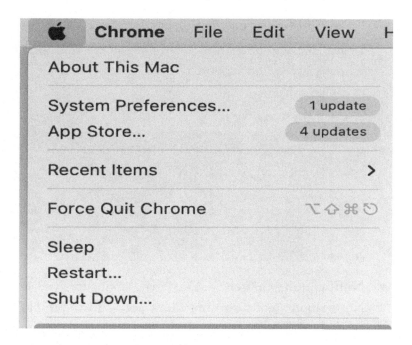

- **App menu** - Immediately below the Apple menu symbol is the presently chosen app menu. When an application is active and in use, you will find categories such as File, Edit, View, Window, and Help. Each application has a unique menu layout.
- **System status menu** - The System status menu contains widgets from the Mac App Store, volume controls, Wi-Fi status, AirPlay, the battery (on laptops), and the date.
- **Spotlight** is Mac's system-wide and web-based search engine. You may enter anything into Spotlight's search bar, and you will almost certainly discover what you're looking for. You can open it by pressing the command+space button.

Q Spotlight Search

- **Siri** - With Siri on the Mac, the personal digital assistant may be used to seek up information, add appointments to the calendar, and make reminders, among other things.
To open Siri:

1)Tap Siri in the Touch Bar (if your Mac has a Touch Bar).

2)Say "Hey Siri" (if enabled in Siri preferences; this option's only available when supported by your Mac, display or headphones).

3)search siri in spotlight

- **Notification Center** - You may configure widgets in Notification Center to offer quick access to the things that are most important to you, including the weather, your daily schedule, iTunes control, and exclusive content from some third-party apps.

How to delete widgets from the Mac menu bar?

Over time, the menu bar can get congested, especially when third-party widgets are added. If you do not use macOS status widgets, you can delete them.

- Control-click or right-click on a Menu bar widget.
- Select Open Settings.
- Uncheck the Show in the Menu bar box.

When you click on the widget in third-party applications (such as Fantastical 2), there is typically a settings icon (that looks like a gear) that you may click to deactivate or disable menu bar access.

How to change the date and the time in the menu bar on the Mac?

Change the date, time, time zone, and appearance of your Mac's Date & Time.

Caution: If you manually change the date and time on your Mac, you may have detrimental effects on apps running on your computer and may be banned from certain games that consider time changes a form of cheating.

How to change the date and time manually

1. Click the date and time in the menu bar located in the upper-right corner of the screen.
2. Click on the link labeled "Open Date & Time Preferences."
3. Select the Time & Date tab.

4. To make modifications, click the lock.
5. Click Unlock after entering your administrator password.
6. Uncheck the option labeled Automatically set date and time.
7. Choose a new date.
8. Choose a new time.
9. You may also automatically set the date and time for a different nation. You can select the United States, Asia, or Europe.

How to change the time zone manually

- Click the date and time in the menu bar located in the upper-right corner of the screen.
- Click on the link labeled "Open Date & Time Preferences."
- Select the Time Zone button.

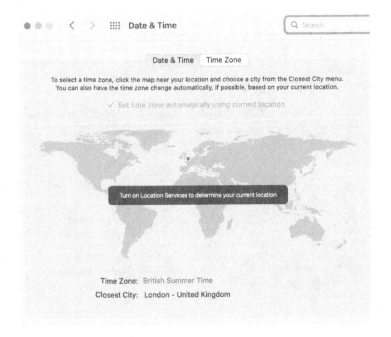

- To make modifications, click the lock.
- Click Unlock after entering your administrator password.
- Uncheck the option next to Set time zone automatically based on location.
- Click a different area.
- How to alter the appearance of the date and time Menu bar widget
- Click the date and time in the Menu bar located in the upper-right corner of the screen.
- Click on the link labeled Open Date & Time Preferences.
- Select the Time tab.
- To make modifications, click the lock.
- Click Unlock after entering your administrator password.
- Click Digital or Analog to modify the appearance of the clock.
- To display the day of the week, check the box next to Show the day of the week.
- Check the box next to Show date to display the date.

How to use the battery icon in the Mac menu bar?

The battery widget in the menu bar, which is exclusive to Apple computers, displays the remaining battery life before you must recharge. It also displays a few interesting statistics regarding your usage.

1. Select the battery icon.

2. The first status indicates approximately how much time remains until the battery dies. In addition, it displays whether

your laptop is using battery power or is hooked up to an outlet.

3. The second status indicates which application is draining the battery. This is useful if you observe that your battery is depleting much faster than usual. It may be an app with bugs.

4. Click Show Percentage to display the remaining battery power as a percentage.

5. Click the Open Energy Saver Preferences button to configure the amount of time your screen and hard drive remain active while not in use.

How to use the spotlight on a Mac?

Spotlight is Apple's system-wide search tool. It will search for applications, documents, files, emails, and more when you enter a search phrase. It also searches the internet, contacts, and maps for directions, converts currencies, performs computations, and much more. It is a one-stop shop for all the shortcuts you use on your Mac.

How to make use of Siri on a Mac?

Siri on the Mac, like Siri on the iPhone and iPad, may serve as your own virtual assistant. It searches for files and folders on your Mac, arranges calendar events, and stores significant search results in your Notification Center. Want to learn something? Siri can assist with this.

How to use the notification center on the Mac?

The Notification Center is a side panel that you may visit whenever you want to quickly view today's schedule, the weather forecast for the afternoon, or your to-do list. Using third-party Notification Center widgets, you may customize your Today display with your most essential productivity applications.

How to change the menu bar icon order?

- Depress the command key on the keyboard.
- Click on the symbol you wish to relocate. Ensure that the command button is still depressed.
- Drag the symbol to its new spot by dragging it.
- Release the mouse and command key to allow the icon to drop into place.

BONUS: PRO TIPS FOR MENU BAR WIDGETS ON THE MAC

When the option key is pressed on the keyboard while clicking on certain menu bar widgets, alternative information is displayed.

- Option + Click on Wi-Fi to get further information about your wireless network, including your IP address, the address of your router, and your security type. Additionally, you may generate a diagnostic report and launch a wireless diagnostic.
- Option + Click on Bluetooth to view further information on your Bluetooth connection, including its address and version. On your desktop, you may also write a diagnostic report.
- Option + Click Notification Center to manually enable or off Do Not Disturb.

Connecting to Wi-Fi Network

Before connecting to your Wi-Fi, the following must be understood:

- Wi-Fi name (SSID)
- Wi-Fi security key, password, or passphrase

Step 1: Click on the AirPort/Wi-Fi icon on the desktop, then pick the Wi-Fi name (SSID) to which you wish to connect.

- Enter the Wi-Fi password when prompted, then click Join.
- Check the Remember this network option if you want your Mac computer to remember this Wi-Fi network and connect to it automatically when it is within range.
- When this icon appears in the menu bar, it indicates a successful connection.
- Utilizing the Network pane to connect

Step 2: On the desktop, pick the System Preferences... option by clicking the Apple symbol.

Click the Network icon in Step 2.

Step 3: Pick Wi-Fi from the left pane, click the Network Name drop-down menu and then select the Wi-Fi network name to which you wish to join.

NOTE: Depending on the version of your Mac, Wi-Fi may appear as AirPort. Enter the Wi-Fi password when prompted, then click Join. Check the Remember this network option if you want your Mac computer to remember this Wi-Fi network and connect to it automatically when it is within range.

Step 4: Click "Apply."

You should now be connected to the Wi-Fi successfully.

Chapter 2: The Basics of the Mac

Basic Settings

While unboxing a brand-new MacBook is definitely thrilling, there are a number of changes, recommendations, and repairs you should perform on Day 1 that go beyond the default MacBook settings. Here are some of my favorite applications that will make your smartphone easier to use.

After you've navigated through the early stages of the Mac Setup Assistant, when you're prompted to enter your Apple ID, connect to a network, etc., consider updating or at least reviewing these settings on your new MacBook.

Check for amendments

Has Apple released a macOS upgrade since it manufactured your MacBook? Click the Apple icon in the upper-left corner of the screen and choose About This Mac to find out. You should be viewing the General tab inside About This Mac. In this case, click the Software Update icon to access System Preferences and check for updates.

Enhanced battery charging

If your MacBook will spend the majority of its time plugged in, you should adjust this setting. MacOS may learn your charging patterns to extend the life of your battery. Select Battery Preferences from the drop-down menu that appears when you click the battery symbol in the menu bar at the top of your display. (If you don't see a battery icon in the menu bar, go to System Preferences > Energy Saver and choose Show battery status in the menu bar.) Select Optimized battery charging at the bottom of the available selections. This will delay charging after the battery reaches 80% capacity.

Set up Siri

By default, Siri should be activated, but if you wish to use Siri just on your iPhone, you may disable Siri by navigating to System Preferences > Siri and deselecting the Enable Ask Siri checkbox. If you want to use Siri regularly, you may customize Siri's voice, language, and keyboard shortcuts from this window.

Modify the Touch Bar

If you have one of the final remaining Intel-based MacBook Pro models with the Touch Bar, navigate to System Preferences > Keyboard, select the Customize Touch Bar option, and then drag the buttons you wish to appear on the Touch Bar's default view to the Touch Bar below the display. Not to fear, they will traverse the hinge from your display to the Touch Bar.

Sync directories through iCloud

Syncing the Desktop and Documents folders between my two Macs and my iOS devices is really beneficial. To synchronize these two folders, navigate to System Preferences > Apple ID > iCloud and select the box next to iCloud Drive. Select the Desktop and Documents directories by clicking Options next to iCloud Drive and then selecting the Desktop and Documents folders.

Choose default browser

Even though Chrome consumes more system resources than Safari, I prefer it since the favicons make it easier to monitor all of my open tabs. To change the default web browser, navigate to System Preferences > General and pick an alternative to Safari as the default web browser.

Set the direction of the scrolling

The "normal" scrolling direction of a MacBook does not feel natural to me. If you wish the two-finger swipe gesture to scroll vertically in the other direction, select the Scroll & Zoom option in System Preferences > Trackpad. Uncheck the item labeled "Scroll direction: Natural next."

Insert and delete objects from the Dock

Apple places a number of default applications in the Dock at the bottom of the display. You may create room in the Dock for the apps you use most frequently by deleting unnecessary ones. To remove an app from the Dock, click and drag its icon to the desktop until the word Remove appears above the icon, and then release. Voila, it has vanished! To add an application to the Dock, launch it and then right-click on its Dock icon, hover over the Options line, and select Keep in Dock.

Shift the Dock

On a widescreen MacBook display, you may find it more useful to have the Dock on the side rather than at the bottom of the screen. To relocate the Dock, choose Left or Right for Position on Screen in System Preferences > Dock & Menu Bar. While there, you can also modify the size of the Dock by dragging a slider. Checking the box to Automatically hide and reveal the Dock will also cause it to disappear while it is not in use.

Display battery percent

Similar to an iPhone, a MacBook shows a little battery symbol at the top of the screen to indicate the remaining battery life. It would be more useful if the remaining battery % was also displayed next to this symbol.

To display the percentage, navigate to System Preferences > Dock & Menu Bar > Battery on the left. Check the box next to Show Percentage, and the percentage should appear in the Menu Bar next to the battery indicator.

Stop autoplaying videos

Safari now combats two of the most irritating aspects of the Internet: autoplay videos and ad trackers. Ad tracking is disabled by default, however, you will need to enable a global setting to prevent autoplay videos.

Click on the Websites tab under Safari's Preferences. Select Auto-Play from the menu on the left and Select Never Auto-Play or Stop Media with Sound at the bottom of the window while browsing other websites and enjoy the silence.

Perform a Night Shift

Before bed, staring at a blue screen might disrupt your body's internal schedule and make it harder to fall asleep. With Apple's Night Move function, your display's colors shift toward the warmer end of the color spectrum in the evening. Click the Night Shift tab inside System Preferences > Displays. You may configure Night Shift to activate from sunset to sunrise, or you can choose a custom time range. Use the slider to modify the effect's color temperature between less and more warmth. Once you begin using Night Shift, you will wonder how you ever endured evenings in front of a frigid, blue screen.

Make your desktop dynamic

Apple created a dynamic wallpaper for MacOS Mojave that gradually changes its lighting throughout the day, from a bright, sunny desert picture during the day to a cool, dark screen at night. Go to System Preferences > Desktop & Screen Saver to locate it.

Although Mojave initially came with only two dynamic wallpapers, Mojave and Solar Gradients, there are now plenty to pick from and sites where you can download more ones.

Try the night mode

MacOS Mojave also included an authentic dark mode for Macs. Go to System Preferences > General to find the Light and Dark settings for Appearance at the top.

On the majority of applications, dark mode makes the backdrop black and the text white. Want both Light and Dark alternatives? When Auto is selected, the buttons, menus, and windows will alter throughout the day.

Set Do Not Disturb hours

Along with blue displays, alerts beyond a particular hour have no place in my household. As with iOS, macOS allows you to mute alerts at night so that you are not interrupted when watching Netflix or sleeping. Select the option labeled Turn on Do Not Disturb from System Preferences > Notifications.

By default, the Do Not Disturb Window is set from 10 p.m. to 7 a.m., but you may customize it. There are choices to enable the function while the display of your MacBook is asleep or when you are mirroring the display to a TV or projector (and presumably watching a movie or show or video). You may also allow calls to come through (if you use your MacBook to accept calls) or merely repeated calls, which may indicate an emergency or anything that requires your immediate attention.

Set app download limit tolerability

If you want to download software from the entire web and not just the Mac App Store, you must instruct MacOS to loosen up a bit. To make changes, navigate to System Preferences > Security & Privacy > General, then click the lock in the lower-left corner and enter your password. Choose App Store and recognized developers under Allow applications to be downloaded from.

<u>Select the rate at which your MacBook locks</u>

On the Security & Privacy tab, you may configure how long your MacBook can be inactive before locking the screen. Setting a longer duration is more convenient, but less secure. You must also specify the amount of time before the screen saver begins, as the timer will not start until the screen saver is activated. By navigating to System Preferences > Desktop & Screen Saver and using the drop-down menu at the top of the window, you can set the design and duration of your screen saver.

Work with Documents

You may generate reports, essays, spreadsheets, financial charts, presentations, and slideshows with macOS applications, such as Pages or TextEdit, or Mac App Store applications.

Tip: If you have concerns about how to use an application such as Pages or TextEdit, select Help from the menu bar while working on the application, then consult the application's user guide.

<u>Create documents</u>

On your Mac, launch a document-creation application (Pages for example).

- Open TextEdit to produce a plain text, rich text, or HTML document, for example.
- Click New Document in the Open dialogue box, or navigate to File > New.

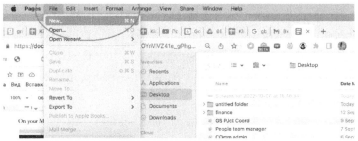

Numerous Mac machines include the following Apple applications for creating reports, spreadsheets, and presentations, among other things:

Create letters, reports, fliers, and posters, among other documents. Pages contain several document templates that make it simple to generate attractive papers. Consult the Pages User Manual.

Create spreadsheets to show and organize your data. Start with a template and alter it to your liking by adding formulae, charts, and photos, among other things. Consult the Numbers User Manual.

Create captivating presentations with photos, videos, charts, and slide animations with Keynote. Consult the Keynote User Manual.

If Pages, Numbers, or Keynote are not already installed on your Mac, you may download them from the App Store.

They are also accessible on iCloud.com and on iOS and iPadOS devices (through the App Store).

Format documents

There are several ways to format and manage text in documents on a Mac:

- Change fonts and styles by selecting Format > Show Fonts, Format > Font > Show Fonts, or Format > Style in a document. See Format text with typefaces in documents.

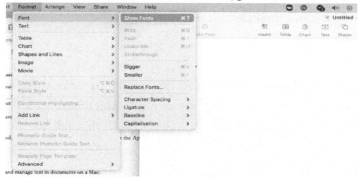

- Change colors by selecting Format > Show Colors or Format > Font > Show Colors in a document. See Use colors in documents.
- Enter many sorts of characters, including those with accent marks and diacritic markings.

- In the majority of applications, spelling is checked as you enter, and errors are automatically rectified. You can disable these features or utilize other choices. See Check spelling and grammar.
- Check definitions by selecting the desired text in a document, Control-clicking it, and selecting Look Up. See Look up words.
- To translate text, pick the desired text in a document, Control-click it, and then select Translate. See Text translation.

Save documents

Many applications on your Mac will automatically save your papers as you work. You can save a document at any moment.

Save a document by selecting File > Save, entering a name, selecting where to save the document (click the down arrow to display more locations), and then click Save.

You may add tags to your saved documents to make them simpler to locate later. You may be able to save your document to iCloud Drive so that it is accessible on your desktops, iOS, and iPadOS devices with iCloud Drive installed.

Save a document under a different name: Choose File > Save As in a document, then input a new name. If Save As is not shown, hit and hold Option, then reopen the File menu.

Save a document as a copy: Choose File > Duplicate or File > Save As in a document.

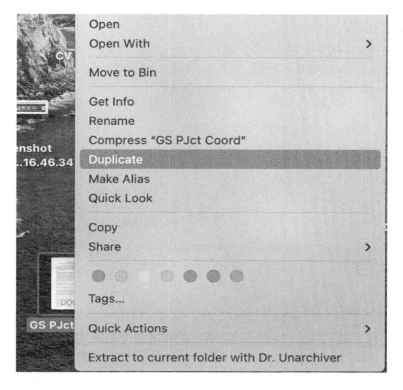

Additionally, you may save a document as a PDF and merge multiple files into a single PDF.

Adding an Email Account on your Mac

Apple's Mail is Apple's application for sending emails. Mail is integrated with macOS, so the application may be found on any Mac. The identical software is also available for your iPad and iPhone. It is an excellent alternative to utilizing a web browser to access your multiple email accounts, including Gmail and iCloud mail. In fact, one of the nicest features of Mail is that you can configure it to receive emails from all of your email accounts in one location, so you only need to use one app and you will never miss another email.

This chapter describes the procedures necessary to configure email on your Mac or MacBook, including how to establish a second email account.

As an introduction, we will highlight a few of the reasons why we use Mail on our Macs.

Here are some advantages of utilizing email:

- You configure Mail to receive emails from all of your email addresses, including your business email and personal email, so that you can read and send all of your emails from the same location.

- It is really simple to set up because it is compatible with popular email services such as Gmail, Yahoo! Mail, Outlook, and, of course, Apple's iCloud. It supports Exchange as well.

- You may add and annotate attachments; for instance, you can email a photo or PDF with "drawn on" instructions.
- It is compatible with other macOS applications, like Calendar and Maps.
- Apple's Mail program will automatically offer the receiver a download link when you send huge files and folders as attachments.
- It is really straightforward to block senders and unsubscribe from mailing lists.
- When group interactions become too distracting, you may silence them.
- You may organize your email messages into Mailboxes that adhere to specific parameters, such as unread, received today, or from specific individuals.
- You may Flag your communications with a distinct color to make it simpler to locate certain groupings of emails.
- It is simple to search through your whole email inbox.

To locate the Mail application on a Mac or MacBook, press Command + Space Bar and begin typing Mail, or select the Mail icon in the Dock.

How to configure Mail on a Mac

Setting up email on a Mac or MacBook is quite simple, especially if you use one of the more popular providers, such as Gmail, Yahoo, or Apple's iCloud. Only your email address and login credentials are required. Here is what must be done:

- Open System Preferences

- Select Internet Accounts.
- You'll see a list of frequently used services on the right, including iCloud, Exchange, Google, Twitter, Facebook, and Yahoo. If you do not see them, please click the plus symbol.

You may also add an email account from within Apple Mail; in fact, the program will encourage you to do so the first time you launch Mail.

- Open Mail.
- Click on Mail in the menu and select Accounts; this will open the same window as accessed via System Preferences.
- If you desire to disconnect or disable any of these accounts, simply pick them and click the minus (-) button on this page.

Media files

Photos

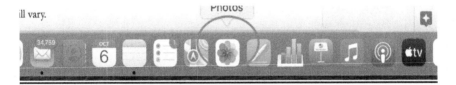

Apple's Photos for Mac has expanded upon the solid foundations established by iPhoto and Photos for iOS to provide you with a quick and practical method to organize, edit, and share all your photographs (without any stress).

In addition, using the Markup editor, you can be quite creative with your memories and design great things!

Whether you're new to photo management apps, upgrading from iPhoto, or researching alternatives to Aperture and Lightroom, here's all you need to know about Photos for macOS!

Starting off with Photos on a Mac

When you initially launch Photos, you are shown an overview of what the app will look like once you've uploaded all of your photos, videos, and memories. You will receive an overview of what to anticipate.

With the Photos app, you can create physical mementos such as calendars, collages, mugs, and more. However, these options are only accessible in the United States, Canada, Japan, and some European and Pacific Asian nations.

The introduction will demonstrate how to arrange and classify your photographs.

Depending on whether you are new to picture management or a veteran iPhoto, Aperture, or Lightroom user, your next steps will vary.

If you're new to organizing pictures on a Mac, do you have folders of disorganized images cluttering your desktop? Have you never used iPhoto or Aperture, Apple's two Mac picture programs? Photos facilitate the transfer of material from your desktop and iPhone to Photos on your Mac and in the cloud.

Once you have completed the basic setup, you can begin by uploading photos and videos or by taking a tour. If you're inexperienced with photos, the tour is your best option!

Upon completion of the trip, you have the option of...

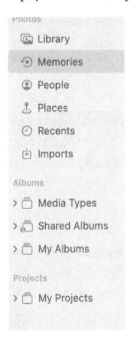

- Connect a camera or memory card to a computer
- Directly drag images into Photos
- Import is accessible via the file menu.
- Enable iCloud Photo Library in the Preferences menu.

... and with that, you are ready to begin uploading photographs!

If you're an iPhoto or Aperture upgrader

Aperture is incompatible with macOS Catalina as of now. You will still be able to use Photos to choose your Aperture library, as seen below, although this may only display the original images and not your adjustments. Apple will release a macOS Catalina update that addresses this vulnerability. You should maintain your Aperture library until then and plan to move it to Photos again.

Apple stated in 2014 that iPhoto and Aperture, its older picture storing and editing tools for the Mac, will no longer get updates. Instead, the company introduced Photos. If you've been fighting the change, but have now chosen to make the switch to Photos on the Mac, you won't experience as much agony as you may anticipate.

If you just have a single iPhoto library on your Mac, the Photos application should upgrade immediately when you launch it. If you need to utilize iPhoto for whatever reason, your old iPhoto library will remain, but updates made to older photographs will not immediately sync with your new photo library.

If you have numerous libraries on your computer, Photos will prompt you to choose which library to import. Unfortunately, many libraries cannot be merged into a single photo library; you must choose which one to use. If this is necessary, you can utilize Aperture to combine libraries and then import the consolidated library into Photos. However, importing an existing Aperture library into Photos is only possible through a manual migration.

Importing pictures and folders into Photos

After setting up Photos, the following step is to import your photos. What you need to know about importing older photos and libraries into Photos for Mac.

- Launch Photos from the Dock or Applications directory.
- Select the File menu.
- Select Import (or type command-Shift-I).
- Locate and choose the image(s) you wish to import.
- Click the Review for Import button.
- Click Import All New Photos in the upper right corner to confirm your photos.

Now, the file has been uploaded to your Photos library.

You may also import photographs from the Finder by dragging and dropping them onto the Photos icon; Photos will import them.

Keep in mind, though, that Photos does not include original photos in imports by default. It maintains connections to them, allowing you to utilize photos to modify or catalog them without moving them.

This is a sword with two edges: It minimizes the size of the photographs' library, but it might be perplexing if your objective is to organize folders and disks containing numerous photos. To ensure that imported files are copied to your photos library, you must set Photos' options to transfer imported files to the photos library. If you intend to share those imported photographs on other devices, there's a second crucial reason to do so: iCloud Photo Library will only upload objects that have been copied to the photos' library.

Instructions for copying imported files to your Photos library

1. Click the Photos icon while Photos is open.
2. Select Settings...
3. Select the Copy to Photos Library checkbox.

This ensures that only objects that have been copied to the library are uploaded to iCloud Photos.

How to import iPhoto into Photos for macOS

If you're switching from iPhoto to Photos for Mac and you've never had more than one iPhoto library on your Mac, the upgrade method is straightforward: Photos will automatically import all of your iPhoto photographs once you use the program for the first time.

If you need to utilize iPhoto for whatever reason, your old iPhoto library will remain, but updates made to older photographs will not immediately sync with your new Photos library. If you no longer use your old iPhoto library, you may dump it - your photographs are now stored securely in Photos (and if you've enabled iCloud Photo Library, in iCloud as well).

If you are using numerous libraries, photos for Mac is compatible with a maximum of one primary library per Mac: This implies that it is not possible to integrate many old iPhoto or Aperture libraries into a single master library.

Therefore, if you have numerous libraries on your computer, Photos will prompt you to choose which library to import when you first run the application. After selecting the desired library, Photos will prepare and import the photographs.

While holding down the Option key and clicking on Photos, a pop-up menu will display.

In the Choose Library pop-up, select the desired Library to open. Tap the Select Library button.

You may still update your other older libraries to separate Photos libraries; you'll simply have to import each one individually by using the Option key before launching the Photos application.

The only difference between these other Photos libraries is that only one may be synchronized with iCloud Photo Library at a time. Your other files will be isolated locally (or externally, if they are stored on a hard drive) from iCloud's sync service.

Videos

QuickTime Player offers on-screen controls for playing, pausing, fast-forwarding, and rewinding music and video files.

Using the playback controls, you can also play a file on an AirPlay-enabled device, display a video in a picture-in-picture window, share a file, and adjust the playback speed.

Open a file

To open a video or music file with the QuickTime Player application on your Mac, you can:

- Click the file twice in the Finder.
- If your films or music files are stored in iCloud Drive, click iCloud Drive in the Finder's sidebar, then double-click the file you wish to access. See You can store documents on your Mac, iPhone, and iPad using iCloud Drive.
- Select a file, then select File > Open File, and click Open.
- Before playing a file with an older or third-party media format, QuickTime Player may convert it.

- You may also open a file you've recently worked on by selecting File > Open Recent.

Invoke a file

The playback controls that display when the mouse cursor is over the screen allow you to play and control a file. You may fast forward and rewind, as well as adjust the playback speed.

1. Launch the QuickTime Player application on your Mac and load a video or audio file.
2. Place the cursor anywhere on the video to display its playback controls. (Audio file controls are always available.)

3. Use the playback controls to play the video or audio file; you can move the controls out of the way by dragging them.
4. If your Mac has a Touch Bar, you can utilize the Touch Bar to control playback.

You may adjust the video's playing speed using the forward and rewind buttons. Click the forward or backward button until the movie is playing at the appropriate pace to adjust the playback speed. The available playback speeds are 2x, 5x, 10x, 30x, and 60x.

Option-clicking the forward or rewind button, while a video is playing, allows you to alter the playback speed in minor increments (from 1.1x to 2x).

You may also select a playback speed before the video begins to play. Click the Share and Playback Speed option, then select Playback Speed and the desired speed.

If you want the currently playing file to display on top of all other windows, select View > Float on Top so that a checkmark appears next to it. Select it again to disable it.

A video with picture-in-picture will be played.

With picture-in-picture, you may play a movie in a resizable floating window, allowing you to view it while performing other computer operations.

- Launch QuickTime Player on your Mac and load a video file.
- Place the cursor anywhere on the video to display its playback controls.
- Click the picture-in-picture button in the controls for playback.
- You may slide the picture-in-picture window to a different screen corner or resize it by dragging any window edge.
- Click the full-screen button or the close button to close the window with window within a window.

<u>Play a file in an endless loop.</u>

You may arrange a video or audio file to play constantly, such that it plays from beginning to end and then begins again.

- Open the audio or video file that you wish to loop.
- Select View > Loop to add a checkbox next to it.

- Click the Play button on the controller for playback.

- Select the command again to disable continuous play; the checkmark disappears.

Navigate a video using timecode

You may modify the playback controls' display to show the elapsed time, frame count, or timecode (depending on the characteristics of the video).

Some media files display an 8-digit timecode (00-00-00-00) in the playing controls, as opposed to the 4-digit remaining time code. The timecode displays source time information for a given frame or recorded moments, such as the recording time or frame number. You may utilize the timecode to travel to a specific frame in a media file while exploring a project.

- Modify the presentation of the playback controls: Select View > Time Display, then select the desired display choice.
- Move to a certain time-coded frame: Select View > Time Display > Go To Timecode, and then input the desired timecode.

Books

If you are an Apple user, the Books application is the best option for reading on your Mac. This is particularly convenient if you also use Books on your iPhone and iPad, as you can resume reading where you left off on your computer.

The Books application on macOS is simple to use, but let's examine how to launch a book and personalize your reading experience.

- Select a book using the navigation on the left. If you connect your iPhone and iPad, you may access a book you've already begun by visiting Reading Now. You may also access all of your books, samples, and PDFs in the Library area. And towards the bottom, you may access one of the My Collections groupings.
- If a book has a cloud icon underneath it, it must be downloaded to your Mac in order to be read. Click the Cloud or the three dots next to it, and then pick Download.
- To open the book, simply double-click on it. The book will open in a separate window that may be customized to enhance the reading experience. Position the pointer at the top of the window to see the toolbar.
- Click the Theme and Appearance icon (aA) on the right to launch a tiny pop-up window.
- You may increase or decrease the font size by clicking the large or tiny A at the top.
- Choose a color for your theme from white, sepia, gray, or black. If you select a dark color, the typeface will change to a light hue automatically, and vice versa.

- You are then able to pick a font style. This is ideal for a novel or manual with basic print in a traditional manner.
- Click the arrow on the right or left, or swipe with your trackpad or Magic Mouse, to turn the pages.
- As you read, the Books app provides extra tools in the toolbar. There are three icons on the left that display the table of contents, bookmarks, and highlights or notes.
- On the right of the symbol for the book's theme and look are icons for sharing the book, searching inside it, and bookmarking the current page.
- To dismiss a book you are currently reading, click the red X in the top left corner of the window. You will then return to the Books window's main screen.

Mac users may access the Kindle app to read books.

The Kindle app is another wonderful program for reading books on a Mac (free in the App Store). This choice is beneficial if you have a Kindle e-reader, utilize the web-based reader, or have the Kindle app on your mobile device. Similar to the Books app, it is possible to sync and continue reading on the Mac.

Step 1: Select a book using the left-hand navigation. In addition to PDFs and collections, you may view all or downloaded books by clicking the corresponding links. Double-click a book to launch it. If required, the book will automatically download.

Step 2: Similar to Apple Books on the Mac, you can personalize your reading experience in the Kindle app by clicking the Aa icon in the toolbar.

- Choose from over a dozen font styles, ranging from basic to formal.
- Size of the font: Use the slider to raise or reduce the font size.
- Choose between Justified and Left-Alignment for the page alignment.
- Select Small, Medium, or Large for the line spacing option.
- Width of the page: Use the slider to adjust the width of the page as it appears in the window.
- Use the slider to modify the display's brightness from dark to light.
- Choose from White, Black, or Sepia for the color mode. The typeface will automatically adjust to a dark or light shade based on the color you select.
- You can pick a single-column, multiple-column, or auto-fit layout option to the right of the appearance icon.

Step 3: To flip the pages, click the right and left Arrows or use your trackpad or Magic Mouse to swipe.

Step 4: As you read, you will see more icons in the toolbar and on the left-hand side.

- On the left side of the toolbar, you may return to the Library, go Back, refresh the page, or Go To a specific location in the book. Mark the current page as a Favorite or click Show Notebook to view highlights or notes.
- On the window's left-hand side are three icons for Table of Contents, Search, and Flashcards.

- To close a book, click Library on the toolbar's left side. Your current reading position is automatically stored.

It is handy to read a book on your Mac during a coffee break, when utilizing reference material, or when accessing a handbook for a project. You may always use both Apple Books and Kindle if you cannot choose!

Music

With the release of macOS Catalina, the Music app for Mac replaced iTunes and consolidated Apple Music and your personal music library into a single area. While the demise of iTunes was somewhat distressing for some, macOS Big Sur has demonstrated that the Music app for Mac will remain.

If you are acquainted with iTunes or the iOS Music app, you will likely find the Music app to be intuitive to use. This is a fast refresher on playing music, organizing your collection, and navigating the Music app for Mac if you are new to the Music app. Thus, your finest Mac may resume playing your favorite music. Here's how to utilize the Mac Music app.

How to play music within the Mac music application

A few taps are all it takes to begin playing music in the Music app; you're off to the races.

- Launch Music from the Dock or Applications directory.
- Click the play button that appears while hovering over the desired album or playlist.
- If you wish to play a certain song, click the album or playlist.
- Click the play button that appears on the album image or track number when hovering over it in the tracklist.

How to view your music collection in the Mac music app

Your music collection is also integrated directly into the Music app. You may explore your full collection by artist, album, or song, as well as view newly added tracks. Even the sorting strategy of your collection may be altered.

- Launch Music from the Dock or Applications directory.
- Click Recently Added in the sidebar to browse recently added albums and tracks (but not playlists) to your collection.
- Click Artists on the sidebar to peruse your library's collection of musical artists.
- Select View from the menu.
- Hover over Sort Albums By.
- Click Title, Genre, Year, or Rating to filter results.
- Click the Ascending or Descending button.
- To peruse your music library by album, click Albums on the sidebar.
- Select View from the menu.
- Select Display View Options

- Click the drop-down menu adjacent to then: to select Title, Artist, Year, or Rating.
- To view your songs, click on Songs. Many would claim that this is the traditional iTunes perspective, dating back over two decades to the initial release.
- By clicking the Name, Time, Artist, Album, Genre, or other category bars, you may organize your music according to these criteria.

How to add music to the Mac music application

- Importing songs into the Music app is comparable to how it was previously accomplished in iTunes.
- Launch Music from the Dock or Applications directory.
- Select File from the Menu Bar.
- Click the Import button.
- Select the desired file or folder to import.
- Click Open.

How to access song and album information in the Mac music app

You may right-click on any track to modify its details (such as the album, artist, and year) if you wish to personalize your collection.

- Launch Music from the Dock or Applications directory.
- Control- or right-click on a song or album.
- Click Get Info.
- If you are modifying several songs, click Edit Items.

- If necessary, modify information under the Details, Artwork, Lyrics, Options, Sorting, and File tabs.
- When editing is complete, click OK.
- You can right-click on tracks in Apple Music to view track details, but you cannot alter the information.

Use iCloud

If you want to get the most out of your Mac, you must use iCloud. Here is how to begin doing that.

iCloud is integral to Apple's ecosystem. When enabled, the service allows the synchronization of data across numerous devices via a secure server. If you use many Apple products, iCloud is an excellent way to keep your contacts and calendar events up to date. And even if you drop your Mac down a well, get it stolen by a monkey, or experience some other misfortune, your data will be stored on a server that is retrievable.

iCloud is an essential feature for contemporary Mac users. So let's examine how to configure and utilize iCloud on your Mac.

How to Create an iCloud Account

If you already have an Apple ID, you may sign in to iCloud through System Preferences > Apple ID and follow the on-screen instructions to configure iCloud. If you do not already have an Apple account, though, you may create one at the same spot on your Mac.

Here are the steps to creating an iCloud account:

- An Apple ID can be accessed by selecting System Preferences > Apple ID from the Apple menu.

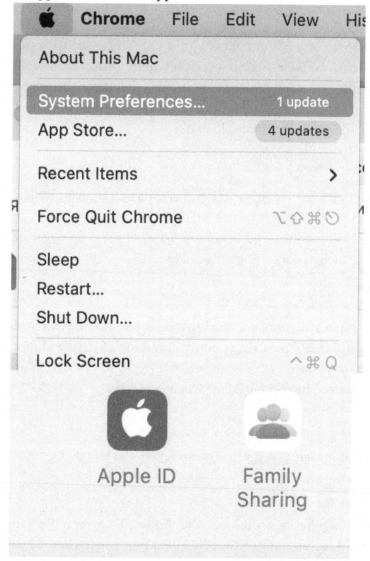

-

- Tap "Create an Apple ID."
- Enter your date of birth, then click Continue.
- Enter your name, email, and password, then click Next. If you don't want to use your current email address, you may establish a new one by clicking Get a free iCloud email address.
- Follow the on-screen directions to complete the installation.

In most countries, the minimum age to create an Apple ID without parental consent is 13. Age restrictions differ by area; thus, you should contact Apple Support for additional information. If a youngster is too young to establish their own account, you can create one for them via Family Sharing.

After creating an Apple ID and completing the verification process, macOS should immediately sign you into your new iCloud account. You will eventually get a window asking if you wish to integrate some data, such as contacts and calendars.

To begin synchronizing the listed data, choose Merge. If you want to select things separately, you may click Don't Merge and proceed with the setup once you've successfully logged in. Find My Mac can also be enabled by clicking Allow when requested.

On your Mac, which iCloud features should you utilize?

After signing in to iCloud, the Apple ID System Preferences will provide a selection of functions that you may enable. If you do not see this list, click iCloud on the sidebar.

The decision on which services to activate boils down to a single question: what information do you wish to sync with iCloud? If you do not utilize some of the above services, you likely do not need to waste storage space synchronizing them. However, the majority of services won't consume a great deal of space, so you may wish to enable them nonetheless.

Let's examine each iCloud function so you can determine which ones are worth activating.

Photos

With Photos enabled, iCloud will synchronize your photos and videos across all of your devices with the service enabled. However, media content can consume a considerable amount of space, so you may need to expand your iCloud storage if you have a large number of items.

Once Photos is enabled, you may modify its settings by navigating to Photos > Preferences > iCloud in the Photos app.

iCloud Keychain is ideal for synchronizing your usernames, passwords, and payment information across many devices in a safe manner. Obviously, you should only enable this capability on devices you fully control.

Cloud Storage

Similar to an online hard drive, iCloud Drive may be used to store other crucial things, such as papers. The service is great for backing up items that you cannot afford to lose, especially if you do not do Time Machine backups regularly.

Clicking Options in System Preferences > Apple ID > iCloud enables you to select which extra files are saved to iCloud Drive. Access iCloud Drive using the Finder's sidebar to manually upload files to the server.

iCloud Mail

By activating iCloud Mail, your iCloud email address is added to the Mac Mail application. Additional settings, including blacklisted senders, signatures, and rules, will sync to the server if iCloud Mail is also chosen in your iCloud Drive preferences.

Notes, Contacts, Calendars, and Reminders

If you own numerous Apple devices, synchronizing your contacts, calendars, reminders, and notes across all of them is quite beneficial. In addition, if something were to happen to your Mac, all of this vital information would still be accessible on the server.

Safari

When Safari for iCloud is enabled, bookmarks, reading lists, and active tabs may be synchronized across several devices. This feature is excellent for facilitating a smooth experience and increasing productivity.

Locate My Mac

Find My Mac enables you to remotely locate, lock, and wipe your Mac. In most situations, there is no valid reason to disable this function. If your Mac gets gone, you will at least have a chance of locating it or stopping a thief from utilizing it.

News Enabling News in iCloud synchronizes some data to the server, including channels, saved stories, and reading history. This function is particularly useful if you read the news on numerous devices.

Enabling iCloud Stocks synchronizes your watch list across many devices.

Home

When iCloud Home is enabled, information about your HomeKit accessories is synchronized to the server for usage on other devices.

Siri

Siri's interaction with you alters its behavior based on your usage. By syncing it to iCloud, you may access your trained and customized version of Apple's artificial intelligence assistant on numerous devices.

Cover My Email and Personal Relay

You may utilize the Hide My Email and Private Relay capabilities if you have an iCloud+ membership, which is essentially a paid iCloud upgrade.

Hide My Email enables you to create a fake email address to use online so that you do not have to reveal your actual information. Using this feature is an excellent method for avoiding spam. Private Relay is a security technology that enables private online browsing. When activated, the service conceals your IP address and other personal data from prying eyes.

Enhancing Your iCloud Storage

If you run out of iCloud storage, you may always purchase extra space. Apple provides a variety of iCloud pricing schemes. Here's how to upgrade your Mac's iCloud storage:

- Select System Preferences > Apple ID from the menu.
- Select iCloud from the navigation bar.
- Click Manage in the window's footer.
- Click Add Storage.
- Select a new storage plan, then click Next to finish the update.
- iCloud is a requirement for modern Mac users.
- If you're a modern Mac user, iCloud is an indispensable and virtually essential utility. Syncing vital information facilitates access from many devices and prevents data loss.

Some iCloud features are more intriguing than others, but the vast majority of users will discover at least one that simplifies their life.

Control Center

The 'Control Center' symbol is located in the upper-right corner of the menu bar. Select the symbol to access the functionality. You will find shortcuts to settings such as 'Wi-Fi', 'Bluetooth', 'AirDrop', 'Do Not Disturb', 'Keyboard Brightness', and 'Screen Mirroring' on 'Control Center'. Click the shortcut to access its configuration. For instance, choosing the 'Wi-Fi' shortcut displays a list of accessible networks from which you may choose.

There are also volume and display brightness controls. Additionally, you may play, stop, and skip items within the "Music" app.

You can drag any shortcut from the 'Control Center' onto the menu bar to set it there. To remove an item from the menu bar, hold down the command key and drag the item out of the bar.

Customizing Mac Control Panel

In macOS Big Sur, Apple offers minimal customization options for the 'Control Center'. You may alter the settings by selecting "Apple" from the menu bar's upper-left corner. Choose System Preferences > Dock & Menu Bar from the menu.

The Control Center item shortcuts are located in the Control Center section. These cannot be deleted from the "Control Center," but their visibility on the menu bar can be modified.

Below the Other Modules section are other Control Center shortcuts that can be added. To add an item, pick it and then tick the 'Show in Control Center' box. Check the 'Show in Menu Bar' checkbox to include the item there as well.

Lastly, beneath the Menu Bar Only section are the keyboard shortcuts that are exclusive to the menu bar. You may add or remove them as necessary.

Notifications & Widget

Since OS X 10.4 (Tiger) in 2005, Apple's macOS has enabled widgets as a part of the operating system. They belonged to the Dashboard application at the time. These mini-applications were shown on a separate desktop. Stickies, weather, and a calculator were among the built-in widgets.

However, in 2019, macOS Catalina eliminated the Dashboard and transferred widgets to the Notification Center.

What Exactly Are Widgets?

Widgets are tiny, self-contained applications that offer limited information and functionality.

In macOS Big Sur, Apple arranged widgets in the Notification Center as a two-column grid beneath any notifications. Each widget may be either tiny, medium, or huge.

You may see widgets by accessing the Notification Center at any moment. If you utilize widgets frequently, it is beneficial to add a keyboard shortcut to this activity.

How to Insert, Delete, and Relocate Apple Widgets

When the Notification Center is active (to Open Notification Centre: Click the date and time in the menu bar, or swipe left with two fingers from the right edge of the trackpad.), an Edit Widgets button appears at the very bottom. This link will launch the editing overlay. This toggles between the view and edit modes. Your existing widget list stays on the right, while a list of available widgets appears on the left.

To add a widget, you may drag it from the available list and place it in the correct location on the Notification Center overlay. Clicking the green plus (+) symbol in the upper-left corner of a widget moves it to the end of the list.

When installing a widget, if many sizes are available, you can select one. MacOS picks the smallest size by default. To use a different size, click the S, M, or L icons underneath the widget prior to its addition.

In edit mode, a widget can be removed by clicking the minus sign (-) in the upper-left corner. In either mode, you can also delete a widget by controlling-clicking and selecting Remove Widget.

Widgets may be moved in either standard view mode or edit mode. Simply relocate a widget by dragging and dropping it.

How to Modify Particular Widgets

Some widgets allow for modification. Those that do will enlarge somewhat when you hover over them while in edit mode. In addition, they will have an Edit Widget label towards the bottom. This button allows you to modify a widget.

Changing the city of the clock widget or choosing a different topic for the news widget are instances of customization.

Which Widgets Can Be Installed on a Mac?

Built-in Widgets macOS allows many widgets for its native applications. The following applications include one or two widgets by default:

- Calendar\sClock\sNews\sNotes
- Photos\sPodcasts\sReminders
- Screen Time Securities
- Widgets From Third-Party Weather Applications
- Many app developers have opted to integrate their own Notification Center widgets, which is permitted. As the new location for widgets on macOS becomes more established, more applications should add support.

Fantastical is a calendar application with a variety of widgets for displaying your events in different ways. They range from a basic glimpse of the current date to widgets presenting a list of upcoming events, a tiny calendar, and the current weather.

Bear, the app for taking notes, provides widgets for displaying a single note and recent notes for a search keyword.

AirBuddy 2 is an application for monitoring battery conditions. It utilizes widgets effectively to display the power levels of your numerous Bluetooth devices.

Utilize Widgets to Quickly Access Vital Information

As part of the Notification Center, Apple makes widgets more accessible than ever before, allowing you to incorporate them into your daily routine. Widgets enable instantaneous access to the most important information on your Mac.

Widgets function optimally in tiny amounts. If you are experiencing information overload, consider reviewing our recommendations on how to maintain concentration.

Use Apple Pay

Using Apple Pay on your Mac mini, you may make purchases on websites in a simple, safe, and confidential manner. Apple does not keep or disclose your Apple Card or other credit or debit card information with merchants using Apple Pay. When shopping online with Safari, look for Apple Pay as a payment option. Use your Magic Keyboard with Touch ID, iPhone, or Apple Watch to confirm your transaction.

Apple Pay and Apple Card are not accessible in all areas or countries. To learn more about Apple Pay, visit Apple Pay. See the Apple Support page Apple Pay Participating Banks for information on current card issuers. Apple Card information may be found at Apple Card Support.

Configure Apple Pay. If you have already set up credit or debit cards on your iPhone or Apple Watch, no additional setup is necessary. You may configure your debit and credit cards under the Wallet & Apple Pay section of System Preferences if you haven't already. Ensure that your iPhone and Apple Watch are logged in with the same Apple ID as your Mac mini.

Purchase items with your iPhone or Apple Watch. Click the Apple Pay button on the website, then use Face ID, Touch ID, or the passcode on your iPhone to authenticate the payment, or double-click the side button on your unlocked Apple Watch. You must be signed in to an Apple Pay-enabled iPhone or Apple Watch with the same Apple ID used on your Mac mini.

You can manage your Apple Card and add or remove payment cards under the Wallet & Apple Pay section of System Preferences.

Chapter 3: Using the Internet

Using Safari and other browsers

Apple has recently added new capabilities to its Safari browser, making the primary Mac application for online exploration speedier and more robust. However, if you desire a change, there are many different browsers available, like Microsoft Edge, Chrome, Firefox, Brave, and many others. This article compiles the finest alternatives to Safari and examines their features.

You may also be interested in learning about DuckDuckGo, which has been published as a browser but is only available to beta testers at this time. We will do an evaluation of the new web browser as soon as we can get our hands on it. In the meantime, read further here: The beta version of DuckDuckGo's privacy-focused Mac browser has been released.

Safari

Apple's Safari browser has been around for a long time, and it has evolved to the point that it is now a pretty strong option for the vast majority of users. It has bookmarks, tabbed browsing, a password manager, private browsing settings, a dark mode, a read later list, and a Shared with You area on the home page that shows links provided to you via Messages.

The reading mode is still one of Safari's best-kept secrets since it transforms every web page into a sleek, distraction-free article.

With the release of macOS Monterey and version 15, Apple introduced Tab Groups, a useful new feature that allows you to group certain tabs by a category of your choice, so you don't have to hunt for them among your other active tabs. This is especially helpful if you are organizing a vacation, or event, or investigating a different hobby. Group Tabs synchronize with Safari on your iPhone, iPad, and other Macs.

Integral to Apple's offering is Intelligent Tracking Protection, which prevents marketers from tracking your activity. This is accompanied by anti-fingerprinting settings that prohibit websites from analyzing your hardware and software setup to determine your online identity, as well as security measures that block potentially malware-infected websites.

Apple Pay is also fully integrated, making it simple to purchase products online using the Touch ID sensor on Macs with Touch Bars or your iPhone. See How to Use Apple Pay on a Mac for further information.

In its current state, Safari is better than ever, and that's before you investigate the various extensions that can expand its powers. The best browser for your Mac is most likely already installed.

Chrome

Chrome remains, by a wide margin, the most popular desktop browser in the world, but this includes Windows users. Chrome is a great tool with a vast ecosystem of plug-ins and extensions, ranging from privacy monitors to ones that correct your grammar, so it's easy to understand why it's so popular.

However, Chrome handles multiple tabs fairly well. Nevertheless, leaving a large number of tabs open at once might result in Chrome hogging RAM. Nonetheless, this is true of most browsers. In operation, it is quick. Pages are produced rapidly and there is a global zoom setting, which might be useful if you find text on current websites to be too tiny. As expected, Chrome integrates seamlessly with Google's web apps, such as Drive, Docs, Calendar, Photos, and Translate, allowing users to activate them from an app tray in the menu bar. You may also use accessible browser extensions, such as

Google Keep, to generate reminders straight from the browser.

Chrome's extensions are what distinguish it from other browsers, and there are over 150,000 to pick from. You may use password managers like Dashlane, the coupon checker Honey, Grammarly, and so much more to improve your writing. To view our favorite Chrome extensions, visit Best Chrome Extensions. Chrome's password storage is safe, and it may save your payment information so that it's easier to make online payments, although Apple Pay is not supported.

Google employs stringent security measures to prevent you from accessing sites containing malware and separates each tab to prevent cross-contamination should you stumble onto something malicious. Obviously, this is Google we're talking about, so when you use Chrome, you'll be providing the firm with your data, including your internet habits, so make sure you're comfortable with that before you start.

Firefox

Firefox

Web browser

Firefox is another veteran that has just received a much-needed polish. There was once a time when this was one of the leading browsers, but time has not been kind to Mozilla's invention, and Google Chrome in particular has been luring users away. This is unfortunate, given the current version of Firefox is sleek, intelligent, and a great alternative to its more prominent competitors.

Mozilla takes privacy seriously and provides a variety of safety features to keep you secure online. Tracking Protection prevents websites from tracking your web activity and gathering data that can be used to display advertisements. There is also ad and script blocking, which accelerates the loading of online pages. There is also a plugin that sandboxes Facebook so that it cannot track your web habits. Regardless of the modifications behind the hood, our experience with the app shows that it is quick and dependable.

Firefox has always been a customizable browser, so make sure to check out the available themes and extensions that can be used to beautify the browser's menu bar or add other functions. By dragging icons onto the menu bar, you may perform a variety of actions, such as emailing links, storing the page to Firefox's Pocket program for later reading, or sending pages directly to your mobile device.

There may not be as many extensions for Firefox as there are for Chrome, but there are many helpful add-ons that allow you to customize Firefox to your liking. Mozilla provides other tools, such as Relay (similar to iCloud Private Relay), which generates email aliases for use while signing up for online services or providing to individuals to whom you do not wish to reveal your actual email address. A VPN that can conceal your location, together with a monitor that checks for password breaches that may have compromised any of your accounts.

Firefox may not be as powerful as it once was, but it still has plenty of life.

Opera

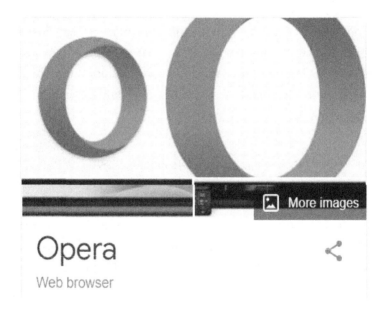

Opera is based on the same foundations as Chrome, which gives it a familiar feel in terms of

performance and functionality. This does not imply that it is only a clone with a different logo, though, since the app's design and tools make it a thoroughly contemporary web browser.

The first is a column on the screen's left with shortcuts to different choices. All of Facebook Messenger, WhatsApp, Telegram, and Instagram can be accessed while browsing the web. There is also the option to add a Twitter account, which is really beneficial if you want to avoid constantly picking up your phone.

My Flow is a feature exclusive to Opera that allows users to transmit web pages straight to their iPhone. Three dots at the bottom of the column launch the settings menu. In this part, you may add or delete many other icons that go to your bookmarks, a news section that compiles the latest headlines from your favorite publications, and a speed dial for frequently visited sites.

In addition to a built-in ad blocker and a free VPN, Opera's privacy features make browsing more convenient. Even though the number of server locations is restricted, the second option is superior for securing public WiFi connections.

Due to Chrome's background, an abundance of extensions are available, as are themes for customizing the browser's appearance. Workspaces, which are effectively the same as Group Tabs in Safari, are now also available. Here, you add new Workspaces (naming them and selecting an appropriate icon) and then opening several tabs within each one. This allows you to rapidly browse between related websites, streamlining your experience and preventing you from having a million tabs open simultaneously.

Opera provides several advantages if you seek a browser that not only protects your online privacy but also lowers the need for other applications on your machine.

Navigate the Internet

<u>Menu bar</u>

Using the mouse, you may access the menu bar positioned at the very top of the screen. When you hold down the mouse button over an item in the main menu, a submenu with more options is "drawn down."

Actions that cannot be carried out are shown in gray or lighter shades of black. The submenus give keyboard shortcuts for numerous frequent activities, allowing you to execute them more quickly than with the mouse.

<u>Address Field</u>

In addition to being situated at the top of the browser window, the address bar features Web navigation buttons and a field for entering the URL of any website or page you wish to visit. The following buttons are featured in Safari's address bar by default:

<u>Command Function</u>

- Back Returns the user to the previous page.
- Forward Proceeds to the following page
- Reload Reloads and shows the current page.
- Add Bookmark Saves the current page's address so you may return to it later.
- You may simply alter the address bar's buttons by selecting View, Customize Address Bar...

A window with buttons that may be dragged to the address bar will appear.

For instance, you may add a home button that, when clicked, will send you immediately to the website you have designated as your home page, or a stop button that will prevent a page from fully loading. You may also drag the default set displayed at the bottom of the window to restore the default setting of the address bar.

The address bar also contains a search box where you can do a Google search for pages and websites containing your search parameters. Click the tiny arrow pointing downwards next to To view a list of past searches, click the magnifying glass symbol in the search field. You will then be presented with a list of your recent searches. If you like, you will find the option to clear recent searches at the bottom of the list.

Status bar

The browser's status bar is situated at the very bottom of the window. When hovering over a link on a web page, the status bar displays the complete URL. Select View, Hide Status Bar if you do not wish to view the status bar.

Scroll bar

The scroll bar is the vertical bar on the right-hand side of the browser window. By placing the mouse cursor on the slider control and depressing the mouse button, you may scroll up and down a web page.

If you have installed the Mac version of Mozilla Firefox, your browser window will have a layout very similar to that described above. To add additional buttons to the toolbar (which is not referred to as the address bar in Firefox), click View, Toolbars, and Customize.

As with Safari, you may drag the buttons you wish to add to the toolbar, or you can click the Restore Default Set button to restore the toolbar to its default configuration.

Firefox for the Mac differs from Safari in that it supports many search engines for doing web searches. It is not exclusive to Google alone. To view a list of available search engines, click the little arrow pointing downwards next to the magnifying glass symbol in the search field. This displays a list of available search engines.

You may also pick Add Engine to access a page on the Mozilla website where you can add more search engines.

Downloading Files

Depending on the sort of thing you wish to store, you may save Safari content to your Mac in a variety of ways. While some internet content cannot be downloaded, files, photos, software, and apps frequently include a dedicated download button. Otherwise, Control-click or double-tap an item to download or save it.

It is advisable not to download software or applications from unreliable sources.

Location of Safari Downloads on a Mac

Downloaded goods from Safari have automatically been placed in your Downloads folder unless you've specified otherwise. To locate this file, use Finder and choose Downloads from the sidebar or press Cmd + Option + L.

If desired, you can alter the location where downloaded files are saved:

- Navigate to Safari > Options.

- Select the Basics tab. Go to the File download location, then select from the menu that appears. If you want additional control over each download, choose to Ask for each download.
- If you wish to choose a specific destination, click Other and choose the folder you want.
- Use Safari's Downloads Button
- You can quickly access your downloads in Safari by clicking the Downloads button, a circle with a downward-pointing arrow, located in the upper-right corner of the Safari window. This will only show if you have recently downloaded an item.

Launch the Downloads Stack in the Dock.

The Dock is another option to rapidly access your downloaded files. Recent downloads are typically stacked on the right side of the dock. You may preview its contents by hovering over it or clicking to enlarge it.

Using Finder, open the Downloads folder.

As previously said, you may also locate Safari downloads using Finder. This is a useful tool for locating stuff on our Mac. Simply click the magnifying glass icon on your menu bar and enter "downloads," or select Finder in your dock to launch the Finder window.

Typically, the Downloads folder may be found on the sidebar, under Favorites.

How to Manage Downloads in Safari

Safari provides many options for managing your ongoing and completed downloads. To perform these operations, launch Safari's Downloads menu. Here are your options:

- Pause Downloads: To pause a download, click the stop button next to the file's name, and then click the restart button to resume the download.
- Find a Downloaded Item: If your Mac is crowded and you cannot locate a downloaded file, click the magnifying glass next to the file's name to open it in Finder.
- To remove a single downloaded item from the list, Control-click the item and select Remove from List. Clicking Clear in the upper-right corner of the pop-up will also erase all recently downloaded goods.

By default, Safari deletes all downloaded files after one day. If you wish to modify this:

- Select "Safari" > "Options."

- Select General, then Remove things from the download list. Choose between After one day, When Safari exits, Upon successful download, and Manually.
- Manage Downloads in Safari

There is a great deal of content that can be downloaded from the Internet, and understanding how to do so is typically half the battle. Then, you can use the suggestions in this article to locate and manage your Safari downloads with ease, including adjusting your download options to have greater control over where your files are saved and when they are erased.

Best Websites for Seniors

While some members of the younger generation believe that older folks and the Internet do not mix, an increasing number of retirees have been comfortable navigating the Internet for at least two decades.

In fact, the majority of those who claim to have invented the Internet (including Al Gore) are of retirement age or older.

And while millions of people use the Internet every day to listen to the newest music, update their social statuses, and for some reason take pictures of the food they're about to eat, there are hundreds upon hundreds of useful websites designed specifically for senior citizens that contain information that can make your life easier, save you money, maximize the benefits you're entitled to, and help you plan for the future.

Here are some of the top online resources for elderly citizens in a variety of fields.

AARP (aarp.org) is the go-to site for anything related to older folks, including money guidance, queries about health benefits, and where to discover savings across the board, regardless of whether you are a member or not. Even better, the website provides advice to everyone who has reached the age of 50 and is beginning to see the end of the road in their journey towards retirement.

The majority of us visit three government websites throughout our lifetimes: the Internal Revenue Service, Medicaid, and the Post Office. Not exactly an enticing recommendation for wanting to see something else administered by the United States government, right?

However, the **Administration on Aging (AOA)** website is well-organized and has a wealth of important information, notably on health and nutrition, as well as the most recent data on aging, free news stories, and an eNewsletter.

ThirdAge (thirdage.com): It seems a little like a video game title, but it's actually a pun on your childhood being your first age, your working years being your second age, and the third age being "healthy living for now and beyond." The site features an excellent Health A-Z encyclopedia that is simply accessible and searchable, as well as articles and blogs on aging well, lifestyle, relationships, and everything else under the sun for today's seniors, as well as the option to attend online classes.

SeniorNet (seniornet.org) was founded in 1986 to give older persons the chance to learn about and utilize computer technology. This not only enables you to keep up with technology as it swiftly alters the way we interact, pay our bills, save our records, etc., but it may also provide you an advantage in maintaining your employment for as long as you choose.

National Senior Persons Law Center (nsclc.org): Among the most difficult aspects of aging is the fact that senior citizens are the primary target of con artists in the United States. Complex systems such as Medicare, wills, estates, retirement homes, and financial investments can be baffling to the elderly, and there are others who prey on the elderly for their own financial benefit, given that our mental faculties tend to deteriorate with age. The National Senior Citizens Law Center (NSCLC) campaigns for senior rights on a broad scale, providing assistance, guidance, and support for a variety of needs.

Buzz 50 (buzz50.com) is an exclusive social network for seniors. Yes! Buzz 50 is a website oriented for adults over the age of 50, particularly recently-retired baby boomers. It offers both discussion forums and chat rooms for seniors to engage with peers not just in the United States but also internationally. Create a profile page and network!

Elder Treks (eldertreks.com): No, it's not supper with William Shatner or tea with Patrick Stewart. Elder Treks enables seniors to organize once-in-a-lifetime journeys that likely wouldn't have been possible during their younger years when job and children responsibilities were of paramount importance. There are both domestic and international destinations, such as Easter Island, the Galapagos Islands, Machu Picchu, Egypt, and Kenya. Activity levels and duration of stay are variable, ranging from a weekend to a month. Obviously, the price tag is a bit steep, but who needs to leave an estate when you can spend 14 days en route to the North Pole aboard the world's largest icebreaker?

Chapter 4: Essential and Popular Apps

AppStore and Installing Apps

An app store (application shop) is an online marketplace for the acquisition and download of software applications.

All of the main mobile operating system providers, including Apple, Google, BlackBerry, and Microsoft, operate their own app shops, giving them control over the applications accessible for their own platforms.

There are also a number of third-party software shops, such as the Amazon Appstore for Android and Cydia for jailbroken Apple iOS devices.

With the emergence of smartphones and tablets, the app store concept gained popularity, but it has now spread to Web browsers and desktop operating systems. Each of the browsers, Mozilla Firefox and Google Chrome, has its own store where users may install Web-based applications. Desktop programs for Mac OS X and Windows 8 are also accessible via app stores.

A related notion is the corporate app store, a portal managed by IT that makes authorized business applications accessible to end users.

Installing applications from the Mac App Store

The Mac App Store is one of the greatest methods for acquiring and installing applications on a Mac. It has benefits and negatives, but the greatest grade is for its usability.

Choose App Store from the Apple menu to launch the Mac App Store. When logged in with an Apple ID, you may download apps: tap Get and then install the app for a free app or one with in-app purchases, or tap the pricing label for a paid app.

If there are in-app purchases, they are listed next to the Get button. You must verify payment by entering your Apple ID and password.

Apple examines each Mac App Store application (and update) before its distribution, thereby limiting the possibility of issues.

The Software Store is also an excellent method for centralizing app updates. In System Preferences > Software Update, you may select to automatically install App Store updates.

How to install Mac applications obtained from external places

Apple sets restrictions on developers, which means that some cannot

– or choose not to – publish their applications on the Mac App Store. The reasons vary, ranging from a lack of Deep system access for utilities to software developers who want the option to send updates without waiting for a Mac App Store review.

If you choose to download program installers over the Internet, you should only do so from trustworthy sources. Download apps from developer websites (such as Intego's) rather than app listing websites.

Unless you've altered your browser's settings, downloaded installers will be stored in /Downloads and come in a number of formats:

- DMG files are disk images that are mountable. Double-clicking a DMG file opens the Finder window. DMGs may contain an installer that must be launched before on-screen instructions can be followed. The majority, however, only include a copy of the software.
  Do not launch the application from within the DMG file; instead, drag it to the Applications folder. A folder shortcut might be given to facilitate this. Unmount the DMG after you're finished by clicking the eject icon next to its name in the Finder sidebar or by Ctrl-clicking within the DMG's window and selecting Eject.

- ZIP files (and very rarely RAR files) are archives that typically contain a single application. Repeatedly, drag the application to the Applications folder before launching it. This helps keep things organized, but certain applications cannot operate unless they are in this folder. (Some will offer to relocate themselves if they are opened in the incorrect area.)

- PKG files are installation packages containing installation-directing scripts and the files to be installed.
  These are often used for applications and utilities that require extra components, system services, and/or files to be deployed elsewhere on your computer and guide you through a multi-step installation procedure. (This is automatic; you only need to click a few times to allow the PKG to perform its function.)

You can remove the DMG, ZIP, or PKG files after installing your software, but if the apps are huge and your bandwidth is restricted, you may want to save them in case you need to reinstall the apps or install them on another Mac.

How to install Mac applications from unofficial app stores

There are various independent alternatives to the Mac App Store. They are often specialized in nature and include a core program that, when launched, allows you to manage which service items are installed on your Mac. Steam is the most popular game shop. It expects you would start buying games from within its app as opposed to /Applications, while it is possible to build desktop shortcuts that may be moved later.

Setapp is a more Mac-like version of a third-party app store. Access to dozens of hand-picked applications is provided for a monthly charge, similar to Netflix. The location of installed applications is /Applications/Setapp. Use Setapp's UI for further administration rather than manually tampering with it.

Clear cautions while installing applications

Upon app installation and activation, your Mac may display security alerts. For instance, if you download an application from the Internet, your Mac will request confirmation before allowing you to use it for the first time. (This is based on the assumption that the Security & Privacy pane of System Preferences is configured to permit applications downloaded from known developers. That is the default; you may change it by clicking the lock, entering your administrator password, and selecting the appropriate radio box.)

Apps may also seek access to your downloads folder, camera, microphone, and other components the first time they are launched.

In certain situations, such as authorizing access to your Downloads folder, you need only click OK on a dialog box. In others, though, such as the above example, you must visit System Preferences to expressly allow permission. These options are stored in System Preferences > Privacy, where there is a whole column for granting or denying access to applications. To grant permission, you must click the lock icon, enter your password, and then tick the corresponding boxes.

There is an option in the General section of System Preferences to permit apps downloaded from the App Store or from the App Store and specified developers. These latter developers have Apple accounts and sign their programs with an Apple-issued certificate to verify their origin.

However, there are situations when you may wish to launch programs from unknown developers. Select the application in the Finder, then right-click or Control-click and choose Open.

If you attempt to open an application from an unknown developer by double-clicking, you may alternatively launch it by navigating to System Preferences > General and hitting the Open Anyway button towards the bottom of the window. This button will launch the application. The button is displayed for approximately one hour after app activation.

After the first time you run an application, you will no longer need to do this; your Mac will remember your preferences.

Launching an Application on Mac

This chapter describes how to start programs from the Dock, Recent Items, and Spotlight in macOS.

Out of the Dock

The lengthy strip of icons at the bottom of Mac's display is known as the Dock. Clicking on applications in the Dock is the most common way to start them. The Dock also displays the state of running programs, such as whether they are active or require your attention.

Dock icons can also display application-specific information, such as the number of unread email messages in Apple Mail, memory resource use graphs (Activity Monitor), or the current date (Calendar).

Apple populates the Dock by default with a few programs. Finder, Mail, Safari (the default web browser), Contacts, Calendar, Photos, and System Preferences are classic examples.

A program may be added to the Dock by dragging its icon from the Finder onto the Dock. The adjacent Dock icons will shift out of the way to create space. Once an application icon appears in the Dock, the program may be launched by clicking on the icon.

Similarly, an app may be removed from the Dock by dragging its icon from the Dock to the Desktop, where it will vanish in a cloud of smoke.

Removing an application from the dock does not remove it.

To remove an application from the dock, Control-click or right-click the application's icon. From the menu that appears, choose Options > Remove from Dock.

From the List of Recent Items

Select Recent Items from the Apple menu (the Apple symbol in the upper-left corner of the screen). Then, all recently utilized apps, documents, and servers will be shown. Choose the item from the list that you wish to access.

This is not a list of often used products, but of recently used ones, a distinction that is minor but significant.

The Windows Start Menu is comparable to the program launcher seen on iOS devices such as the iPhone and iPad. Clicking the Launchpad icon in the Dock (usually the second icon from the left, unless you've customized the Dock) reveals a layer with huge icons for all the programs installed on your Mac. You may move them around, organize them in folders, and rearrange them in any way you see fit.

When an application icon is clicked, the corresponding program is launched.

Not able to locate Launchpad in the Dock? Simply drag it from the Applications folder to the desktop.

In the Applications Directory

The quickest and easiest approach to running an application is to open the Applications folder and click on the desired application.

To locate it, launch the Finder from the Dock (it's the first icon on the left).

Clicking on a vacant area of the desktop is another method for launching the Finder.

Choose Applications from the Finder's Go menu, followed by the app you wish to launch.

Using Spotlight on macOS allows you to search for an application by name and run it using Spotlight, an integrated search system available from different locations.

Spotlight is most easily accessible via the menu bar, which runs along the top of your screen. When the magnifying glass symbol is clicked, the Spotlight search box will appear.

Enter the full or partial name of the program you wish to locate, and Spotlight will display the results as you type. Double-click a program from the resultant drop-down menu to launch it.

How to Maintain an App Icon on the Dock

macOS will add the application's icon to the Dock if you run it from a location other than the Dock, such as the Applications folder or the Recent Items list. This is just temporary, since the icon will be removed from the Dock when the application is closed.

Control-click or right-click the application's icon in the Dock while the application is running to keep it there. From the menu that appears, choose Options > Keep on Dock.

Closing and Uninstalling an Application on Mac

Depending on the application, removing it from macOS is as simple as dragging the. The app bundle is placed in the "Bin" However, this does not completely delete the application. If any preference files are left behind,

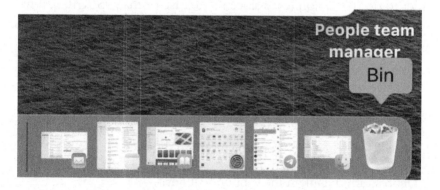

Permanently removing a program is the recommended course of action if you are attempting to eliminate a corrupt or outdated component. If you want to clear up space on your Mac's hard disk, you also need to do a thorough uninstall. Even when reinstalling software to update a serial number, it is often necessary to first uninstall the previous program.

Okay, this approach is not for the slothful, as it needs some effort. Some strong applications have a propensity to trash your macOS with files in many "/Library/" directories. For this stage, you must be familiar with any names that might be related to the app or applications that will be deleted.

To delete programs from your Mac without leaving traces, you must scan the aforementioned directories for files related to the applications. Take the time to browse through each folder for the application's name and developer. Again, this method is NOT for the slothful.

Obviously, you must know how to access your "Library" folder in order to do this action (ever since the release of macOS X 10.6, it has been hidden, but you should have no trouble unhiding it if you follow the next steps).

1. Open your "Finder." (Cmd+space)

2. Click "Go" when the drop-down option displays.

3. Depress and maintain the Option/Alt key.

4. You will find the "Library" option in the drop-down menu between "Computer" and "Home." Click "Library" to access the directory.

5. Examine the presented list of directories to locate those related to the apps to be removed.

6. After that, use "Finder" to access the "Application Support"

folders. Then, look for the directories that hold the data of the uninstalled applications.

There is something more worth mentioning. Additionally, you can discover leftover files in this directory: /Documents/. The majority of software migrated from Windows preserves files in this subdirectory. The same holds true for games ported from Windows to macOS.

Windows programs always save user files in the "Documents" folder. Therefore, when Windows apps are ported to Mac, this behavior is carried over as well.

Lastly, there are hidden directories. By pressing "Command" + "Shift" + ".", you can quickly discover hidden folders in your home directory and determine if they contain any leftover files. Delete any files from the home directory.

How to Close or Force Quit Mac Applications

Force-quitting an application on a Mac may be required for a variety of reasons, the most common being frozen applications. Sometimes you must use sheer force to shut and restart these applications in order to restore their functionality.

Apple is well aware of this, which is why it has provided a variety of solutions for closing recalcitrant applications. You may utilize keyboard shortcuts, third-party applications, and more. One strategy will undoubtedly appeal to you more than the others, but they are all as effective. First on the list is the quickest approach.

Option 1: Macintosh Shortcut

This procedure is very simple and quick. You can force close many applications in a couple of seconds using only your keyboard.

1. Press "Option" + "Command" + "Esc (Escape)".

2. Select the problematic application in the "Force Quit" window that displays.

3. Click the "Force Quit" button.

Option 2: Apple Menu

Using the "Apple Menu" is a more usual way to exit all applications on a Mac. It is just as effective as the shortcut, if not slightly more user-friendly.

1. Open up your "Finder".

2. Go to the menu bar at the top of the page.

3. Click the "Apple" icon placed in the bar's upper-left corner.

4. Select "Force Quit..." from the option that displays.

5. A list of your apps will appear in a new window titled "Force Quit Applications." Select the stalled program and select "Force Quit." That is all. The objective has been attained.

Option 3: Activity Monitor

Windows offers "Task Manager," and Apple has a comparable application. The name of this feature is "Activity Monitor." You may use it to monitor your programs, the performance of your Mac, services, and processes. You can even accomplish much more than this. However, accessing and terminating your programs is a breeze.

1. To display the menu, press "Command" + "Space" on your keyboard. You may also click "Spotlight" in the upper-right corner of your Mac's display.

2. In the "Spotlight Search" field, enter "Activity Monitor."

3. Click "Enter" when you see "Activity Monitor" highlighted.

4. Proceed through the "Activity Monitor" processes list while choosing the frozen applications. The left-hand corner will display "Forcing a process to exit." Click here. All done.

Mostly used Apps

The finest Mac apps let you get more out of your Mac by expanding on its capabilities and shoring up shortcomings. They make it easier and more enjoyable to use your Mac, boosting your productivity and helping you get more out of your device.

With that in mind, we've put together this list of our top programs to install on a new Mac. Whether you just purchased a sleek new 24-inch Apple iMac 2021 or are looking for some new tools to complement your dependable MacBook Air 2020 (which is still one of the best MacBooks available), these applications will help you get the most from your Mac.

Many of these apps are freely available on the Mac App Store, which you can access by clicking the App Store icon on your Mac's dock (if you can't find it, you can also open the Apple menu in the top-left corner and launch the App Store from there).

Because the App Store has hundreds of programs of varying quality, we relied on our own hands-on expertise and user evaluations to compile this list of the finest Mac apps available.

Best Mac productivity apps

Bear

Bear is a free note-taking app that's versatile, encrypted, and easy to use. While Apple continues to make significant improvements to its own free Notes app, Bear performs many of Notes' functions more efficiently and with a greater emphasis on your privacy.

The free version of Bear lets you write notes and to-dos in portable Markdown, organize notes with nested tags, pull assets (like images or text) from web pages into your notes, and even draw or dictate notes using a stylus (for drawing) or Apple Watch (for dictation).

If you subscribe to the upgraded Bear Pro version ($14.99/year) you get even more useful features, like the ability to sync notes between devices, encrypt individual notes with a password, or lock the Bear app with Face/Touch ID.

Fantastical

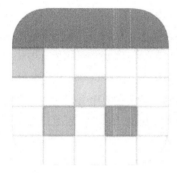

Calendar by Fantastical [4+]
Reminders & Todo List
Flexibits Inc.

★★★★★ 3.8 · 13.4K Ratings

Free · Offers In-App Purchases

Sure, your Mac already has a built-in calendar, but Fantastical does it better. This award-winning app has long been a favorite of ours. The free edition of Fantastical includes a beautiful, easy-to-use calendar that makes it easy to manage your chores and see what's coming up with a quick glance. If you're willing to pay a monthly fee, you can subscribe to the upgraded version that offers more useful features, including cross-platform Fantastical access and syncing across Mac, iPhone, iPad, and Apple Watch.

Spark

Spark Mail – Smart Email Inbox [4+]
Mailbox organizer & calendar
Readdle Technologies Limited

★★★★★ 4.7 • 64.7K Ratings

Free · Offers In-App Purchases

You can do better than the default Mail app on macOS, and Spark is one of the best alternatives. This free email client offers a number of handy features the competition doesn't, including a suite of tools that make it easy for multiple people to manage an inbox by doing things like assigning emails to each other or composing emails collaboratively in real-time. It also offers excellent tools for organizing your inbox, scheduling emails, and finding exactly the message you're looking for using a natural language search engine. You can also find stellar Spark clients on iOS and Android, making it a great tool for managing email across multiple devices.

Best utility apps

Alfred 4

Alfred 4 is the latest and greatest version of Alfred, a better way to search for files on your Mac and the web at large. But Alfred is more than a search tool: you can use it to launch apps, look up spelling and definitions, do quick calculations, and generally make the most of your new Mac. The best part? It's free, though you can pay a one-time fee to buy a license and upgrade to a version with more powerful features, including the ability to play music from iTunes, create workflows and hotkeys, customize Alfred's look, and more.

Daisydisk

DaisyDisk [4+]
Recover disk space
Software Ambience Corp.

★★★★★ 4.6 • 767 Ratings

$9.99

DaisyDisk is one of the best Mac disk space managers because it is powerful, flexible, and aesthetically pleasing. This $10 app will quickly scan your storage drives to show you a gorgeous interactive map of how your Mac's storage space is being used, and its drag-and-drop tools make it easy to quickly move files around and clear up some space. In addition, the most recent release now supports scanning drives on cloud storage services such as Dropbox, Google Drive, and others.

Meeter

Meeter is a handy little app that sits in your Mac's menu bar and organizes all your video calls in one place, whether they be on BlueJeans, FaceTime, Google Meet, Microsoft Teams, Webex, Zoom, or about thirty other video-conferencing platforms. In normal times Meeter is perfect for distant workers, but during the COVID-19 epidemic, it's a beneficial software for everyone who often jumps on video calls with family and friends. The free version connects to your calendar and automatically pulls in details for your upcoming calls, making it easy to quickly see what you have coming up and join with a single click — no more rooting through your email to find the right meeting link.

Best Mac video or photo editing apps

CleanShot X

CleanShot X is a turbocharged screen-capturing tool for Macs, and if you spend a lot of time capturing pics or videos of your desktop it's a real-life-changer. The basic version costs $29 and gives you a more powerful suite of screen-capturing tools that make it easy to quickly snap a pic, edit or annotate it, combine it with other screenshots, and share it with whoever you need to via drag-and-drop.

You can also record video of your screen (even while scrolling) with the option to capture your clicks, your keystrokes, or your webcam, then quickly upload that recording to the cloud or turn it into a GIF. Upgrade to the $8/month Pro version for unlimited cloud storage (the basic version gives you just 1GB), custom domain and branding options, and more.

Pixelmator Pro

Pixelmator [4+]

Pixelmator Team

#16 in Photo & Video

★ ★ ★ ★ ★ 3.7 • 893 Ratings

$4.99

Pixelmator Pro, which costs $40, is not the cheapest photo editing app on the App Store, but it is one of the best. As of this writing, it offers more than 50 image editing tools (including a full set of vector tools), including some pretty neat options like photo editing tools that tap into the power of machine learning. It's a strong competitor to Adobe Photoshop, with the added bonus that you only have to pay for Pixelmator Pro once, whereas Adobe wants to charge you a monthly subscription fee to use its best photo editing tools.

iMovie

Apple's own iMovie isn't the most robust or professional video editor on the market (those honors go to expensive software like Adobe Premiere Pro and Final Cut Pro), but it's one of the easiest to use. Moreover, it is free, whereas the majority of full-featured video editors cost $100 or more. Since iMovie is Apple software it may well already be installed on your Mac, but if not, you can easily grab it from the App Store to do some quick video editing at up to 4K resolution.

Best Mac social media apps

<u>Grids</u>

Grids: Giant Square, Templates [4+]

Cut photo for Instagram layout

TapLab

Designed for iPad

★★★★★ 4.6 • 21.3K Ratings

Free · Offers In-App Purchases

Sure, you can log into Instagram via your web browser of choice, but it's not exactly the most ideal way to browse the image-sharing service. Enter Grids, a free app that makes browsing Instagram on your Mac a much more enjoyable experience. It has a good, clean design that loads quickly, and you can use it to view Instagram photographs and videos in a number of layouts. There's also a handy enlarged view mode for when you want to zoom in. Some of the standard Instagram features (such as the ability to direct messages to other users and view their stories) are only available in Grids if you subscribe to the Pro version, which costs $2.50/month on a month-to-month basis or $1/month on an annual basis.

Tweetbot

Tweetbot for Twitter

A Twitter App with Personality

Tapbots

★★★★★ 4.5 • 4.5K Ratings

Free · Offers In-App Purchases

If you use Twitter frequently, Tweetbot is a must-have app for Mac. This $10 app makes the experience of using Twitter much more enjoyable by giving you access to a powerful suite of filters that can help you block out spoilers, sponsored tweets, and more. It has a sleek user interface that makes it simple to track hashtags, switch between accounts, and add private notes to user profiles.

Best Mac entertainment apps

Spotify

If you're not already using Apple Music to kick out the jams, chances are good you're a Spotify user. Even if you aren't yet, Spotify makes it easy to set up a free account and start listening to your favorite musicians, and the macOS desktop client provides you more control over your playlists than the online app in a clean, easy-to-navigate interface.

Steam

Steam Link [17+]

Stream Your Steam Library

Valve

★ ★ ★ ★ ★ 3.0 • 115 Ratings

Free

If you want to play games on your Mac, it's a good idea to download Steam. Launched by Valve nearly two decades ago, Steam has grown to become one of the biggest PC game platforms in the world. Not every game on Steam is compatible with macOS, but Steam makes it easy to filter through its 50,000+ games to see which ones run on Macs. There are lots of amazing options too, including everything from Sid Meier's Civilization VI and Stardew Valley to Cuphead, Hades, Disco Elysium, and more. Plus, you can connect a compatible Bluetooth controller for some old-fashioned gamepad gaming on your new Mac.

VLC

If you need to play a video file but are uncertain whether Apple's QuickTime player will support it, VLC is the first media player you should download. It's one of the best media players on the market because it supports so many different types of multimedia, including

DVDs, audio/video CDs, and file formats like Xvid, DivX, Real Video, and more—including Ogg Vorbis, a personal favorite. The best part? It's free, open-source, and available across multiple platforms, including iOS.

Chapter 5: Troubleshooting, Tips, and Tricks for Seniors

Use your Mac with other devices

Utilize a keyboard and mouse or trackpad on multiple devices with Mac's Universal Control

With Universal Control, you can work across up to three devices (for example, a Mac and an iPad) using a single keyboard and mouse or trackpad. Additionally, you can drag items between devices.

To utilize Universal Control, make sure of the following:

You're utilizing supported models of Mac and iPad.

Your Mac has macOS 12.3 or later, and your iPad has iPadOS 15.4 or later.

All of your devices are signed in with the same Apple ID using two-factor authentication using the same Apple ID.

You have Wi-Fi, Bluetooth, and Handoff switched on in System Preferences (on your Mac) and in Settings (on your iPad) (your iPad).

Connect your Mac to another Mac or iPad to use Universal Control

With Universal Control, you can establish a connection between your Mac and a nearby device, and then use a single keyboard and mouse or trackpad to work across the devices.

Note: If you haven't used Universal Control in a while, you may need to re-establish the connection.

Do one of the following:

1. Utilize your Mac's mouse or trackpad to move the pointer to the screen's right or the left edge. When a border appears at the edge of Mac's screen, the pointer must be moved past the border until it appears on the other device.
2. On your Mac, choose Apple menu > System Preferences, click Displays, click the Add Display pop-up menu, then choose a device below Link Keyboard and Mouse. Utilize your mouse or trackpad to move the pointer beyond the Mac's screen's edge until it appears on the other device.
3. On your Mac, click Control Center in the menu bar, click Display, then choose a device below Link Keyboard and Mouse. Utilize your mouse or trackpad to move the pointer beyond the Mac's screen's edge until it appears on the other device.

The direction in which you move the pointer while establishing the connection decides which side of the display you use to connect your devices.

You can adjust this by changing the arrangement of the devices in Display preferences. Click on the image of the display, then drag it to the desired position. You can set your Mac to automatically reconnect to any nearby Mac or iPad. Choose Apple menu > System Preferences, click Displays, click Universal Control, then select "Automatically reconnect to any nearby Mac or iPad."

Disconnect your Mac from another device

After you establish a connection between devices using Universal Control, the connection remains until either of the devices goes to sleep or you disconnect them. On your Mac, open the Apple menu > System Preferences, then click Displays. Select the device you wish to disconnect by clicking the Add Display pop-up option.

Turn off Universal Control

You can disable Universal Control to prevent your Mac from connecting to external devices in order to use a keyboard, mouse, or trackpad.

- On your Mac, open the Apple menu > System Preferences, then click Displays .
- Click Universal Control, then do one of the following:
- Turn off all Universal Control connections: Deselect the "Allow your pointer and keyboard to move between any nearby Mac or iPad" checkbox.
- Prevent a connection when moving the pointer to the edge of the screen: deselect the "Push through the edge of a display to connect to a nearby Mac or iPad" checkbox.

Talk to Siri

Siri on the Mac with macOS Big Sur delves much further into your program than it does on iPhone and iPad. It can search for files, examine your system settings, and understands contextual language, allowing you to ask a question and then immediately ask a related one.

How to activate Siri on Mac

When you initially set up your Mac or update to a new version of macOS, you will be prompted to enable Siri on your Mac. If you did not activate it initially, you may do it manually from System Preferences at any time.

- Click the Apple symbol in the upper-left corner of the display.
- Select System Preferences from the drop-down menu.
- Select Siri.
- To speak with Siri, check the box on the left side of the window.
- Select a language.
- Select a Siri Voice.
- If you don't want Siri to speak, turn off Voice Feedback.
- Choose either the internal Mic input or an external accessory for the Mic input.

How to activate "Type to Siri" on a Mac

In macOS High Sierra and later, you can type your search query to Siri instead of having to ask it out loud. So if you're in a meeting and your boss just asked you for a spreadsheet, you can ask Siri to retrieve it for you without interrupting the conversation.

How to activate Siri with a keyboard shortcut

You may access Siri through the app Dock or the Menu bar at the top of the display. But if you prefer keyboard shortcuts, you're in luck — Siri likes them, too.

- Click the Apple symbol in the upper-left corner of the display.
- Choose System Preferences from the menu drop-down.
- Select Siri.

Under Keyboard Shortcut, choose a keyboard shortcut to utilize. By default, you hold down Command-Space, but you can also choose Option-Space, Function-Space, or any other key combination of your choosing.

When a keyboard shortcut has been configured, you may press and hold the two keys until Siri appears.

How to use Siri on Mac with Airpods or supported beats headphones

If you have your AirPods or a set of Beats headphones that feature voice-activated Siri (currently just the Powerbeats Pro), you may call on Siri for help.

- Click the Apple symbol in the upper-left corner of the display.
- Choose System Preferences from the menu drop-down.
- Select Siri.
- Mark the Listen for "Hey Siri" on the headphones checkbox.
- If you want Siri to be activated by voice while your Mac is locked, select the Allow Siri when locked checkbox.

How to pin Siri results to the notification center

You can pin all Siri search results directly to the Notification Center. This may be quite useful if you need to keep track of documents for business, or if you want to add photos of Oscar Isaac to your Today display.

- To activate Siri, click the Siri icon in the menu bar or dock, or use the corresponding keyboard shortcut.
- Tell Siri to find you a file, or document, or perform a web search.
- Click the Plus (+) button next to the search results when they display in Siri's window.

- The results of Siri searches will be pinned to the Today view of the Notification Center. To delete it, hover over the search section of the Notification Center and click the X.

Back up your Files

You may have stumbled onto this page because you recently experienced the horrible scenario of your Mac failing without a backup, or because you know someone who has experienced such a tragedy and want to prevent it from happening to you.

Or perhaps you messed up a document you were working on, saved over something you didn't want to lose or realized you accidentally deleted a substantial amount of work. Recovering unsaved or lost Word documents might provide unique difficulties. If only you had a backup and could recover an earlier version.

Regardless of why you want to learn the best way to back up your Mac, we want to assist you in developing a backup strategy. We will examine the different types of Mac backups, such as local wired or wireless backups, live backups, remote backups, and online backup.

We'll also examine the best Mac backup solutions, including backing up to iCloud or another online service such as Dropbox, using Time Machine or other backup software for a local backup (we have an in-depth article about how to use Time Machine here), and the various remote backup services that are available to you if you want to make sure that you can recover your data if both your computer and local backup gets wiped out.

If you have just lost everything on your Mac due to a damaged drive, read this article for suggestions on how to retrieve your data from the damaged drive.

Ten reasons why you should back up your Mac

We're probably preaching to the choir here, but here are a few reasons why you should absolutely back up your Mac, in no particular order:

1. Because you (or another person) may accidentally spill a drink on your Mac.
2. Because your drive could fail and SSDs are notoriously difficult to recover data from.
3. Because you may lose your Mac or someone might take your Mac.
4. If you encounter Mac malware, a backup will allow you to retrieve your data before the infestation.
5. Before installing a major macOS update, you should back up your Mac in case something stops working and you need to revert to the previous version of the operating system.
6. You will be able to access old papers and previous versions of documents.
7. You may believe there is nothing on your Mac that needs to be backed up – perhaps you sync everything in iCloud – but

we promise you will miss something if you erase your Mac and expect to restore everything to its original state.

8. It makes setting up a new Mac very straightforward. You may quickly restore all your data onto a new Mac and continue as if it were the same computer.

9. It means you could access your data from another Mac if necessary.

10. Some things, like images, are difficult to replace or reproduce so be sure they are preserved carefully.

Best backup method for a Mac

There are numerous methods for backing up a Mac, but if you had to choose just one, which would you choose?

Time Machine, Apple's free backup software, is likely the easiest and most cost-effective alternative. The only related expense would be acquiring an external drive but given you can get 1TB storage for less than £40/$30 these days, it shouldn't break the bank. We've got a round-up of the best hard drives here.

Time Machine is an excellent backup option, but is it the best? A solution that is not stored in the same area as your Mac may be preferable, considering that a fire or water might destroy both your Mac and its backup.

There are other alternatives to Time Machine that you may find more suitable. We examine the finest backup software, including Acronis, ChronoSync, Carbon Copy Cloner, Carbonite, and SuperDuper, individually.

Option 1: Utilize Time Travel

Apple offers Time Machine, its own backup program, as part of macOS. It is a very user-friendly solution. Plug in an external storage device, such as a hard disk or solid-state drive, and begin Time Machine backups. We have a comprehensive guide for backing up your Mac with Time Machine.

Time Machine will generate a versioned backup of your Mac, which means it will save hourly backups for the previous 24 hours, daily backups for the previous month, and weekly backups for each month. You can thus retrieve a prior version of a document if necessary.

Not only does having a versioned backup protect you if something goes wrong with your Mac, but it also protects you against human mistakes (saving over a document for example). ChronoSync ($49.99/£36.00 at Econ Technologies) is also capable of creating versioned backups.

Additionally, Time Machine's strong integration with macOS is a plus. A Time Machine backup facilitates the transfer of all data, settings, and applications from one Mac to another. It is also really easy to use.

Time Machine's only significant drawback is that you must remember to connect in your hard drive, or else nothing will be backed up. However, you can set up Time Machine on a NAS drive for a wireless backup, but it may be a bit slower. You'll also need a substantial amount of storage because Time Machine incremental backups consume more space than the entirety of your Mac's data. We recommend utilizing a storage device with at least four times the capacity of your Mac. View our selection of the best hard drives.

How to create backups with Time Machine

Here is a step-by-step guide to backing up with Time Machine, but the essential steps are as follows:

- Connect hard disk or solid-state drive (alternatively you can use a NAS drive).
- You should notice an alert on your Mac asking if you wish to utilize the drive with Time Machine. Select Use as Backup Disk from the menu.
- If you do not notice the warning, ensure that the disk is formatted appropriately; it must be formatted as Mac OS Extended (Journaled).
- If you still don't see the notice, visit System Preferences > Time Machine and pick Backup Disk.
- Choose the storage device and click Use Disk.

Option 2: Use iCloud

With iPhones and iPads, you may use iCloud to save a backup of your device from which you can restore it. If you purchase a new iPhone, you may restore all of your settings and data using iCloud backup.

If you hoped to back up your Mac to Apple's iCloud instead of an external hard drive, you'll be disappointed: you can't back up your entire Mac to iCloud, and iCloud is incompatible with Time Machine. However, iCloud may still be utilized to back up a portion of your Mac's data.

You can automatically sync certain files from your Mac to iCloud; however, you should not consider this a backup, as there will be no previous version of the file if you delete or modify it. This is a synchronization, not a backup. However, having your files synchronized to iCloud is advantageous since you can access them from any Apple device (and even from a PC if you go via iCloud.com).

Included among the files that may be synchronized in this manner are all files on your Desktop and in your Documents folder. If you use applications such as Pages and Numbers, your documents will be saved to the cloud, and your Mail and Messages can also be kept in the cloud.

Apple requires a monthly membership fee for iCloud storage. Monthly subscription costs are as follows:

- UK: 79p (50GB), £2.49 (200GB), £6.99 (2TB)

- US: 99c (50GB), $2.99 (200GB), $9.99 (2TB)
- Euros: 99c (50GB), €2.99 (200GB), €9.99 (2TB)
- If you subscribe to Apple Music (£9.99/$9.99 per month), you can utilize iCloud Music Library to access your music from anywhere. Here, we distinguish between iTunes Match and Apple Music.

That's what you can sync automatically, but as we noted above, you can utilize iCloud to back up some of the data on your Mac merely by transferring it to your iCloud Drive.

Here is how to synchronize your Mac with iCloud.

- On your Mac, launch System Preferences and select iCloud.
- If you haven't already, sign in to iCloud.
- Check the box next to iCloud.
- Select the Options checkbox within the iCloud row.
- Check the box next to anything you want to keep in iCloud, including your Desktop folder, Pages documents, and System Preferences.
- How to make an iCloud backup of your Mac
- This will not be automated in the same manner as the sync, but it is a good idea to periodically copy any non-synced data to iCloud. This is how to accomplish it:
- Launch the Finder.
- Click on the iCloud Drive folder in the left-hand navigation bar.
- Open a second Finder window and search for any folders, files, or data linked with a non-cloud-based application.
- This information may now be copied to your iCloud Drive.

- Now you will not only be able to access the data on any of your Apple devices, and even via the web on a non-Apple device, you will be able to recover it if something goes wrong with your Mac. It is also an excellent method for obtaining an offline backup.
- Just don't forget to routinely update that 'backup'.

Option 3: Use a different cloud backup service

If you are looking for a way to sync and share files, there are numerous alternatives to iCloud. You could already be using Dropbox, Google Drive, Microsoft OneDrive, or one of the other Cloud storage options we look at here.

Rather than backing up all of your data, these solutions are typically employed for sharing files with coworkers or friends or storing files that everyone can collaborate on. You may subscribe to data plans that allow you to save all of your data in the cloud, similar to iCloud, but you would not be able to readily download a clone of your Mac if it were lost.

How to back up your files to Dropbox, OneDrive, or Google Drive

If you need to back up a few files, Dropbox, One Drive, or Google Drive may be a suitable option. You'll have the benefit of being able to view the files from any device and you will effectively have a low-cost off-site backup.

- In the case of Dropbox, sign up for an account on this page, then download and install the program. (Or sign in to your current account if you're already a member.)
- Once the program has been installed on your Mac, launch Dropbox to access the web interface where you may copy your files.
- Click Upload Files or Upload Folder on the right, go to the folder you wish to upload, and then click Choose. Wait while the folder uploads.
- Additionally, you may drag and drop your files and folders into Dropbox using the Finder. When DropBox is loaded on your Mac you will see a Dropbox tab under Favourites in the Finder, just drag and drop anything into that folder and it will be backed up to Dropbox, and available on any other computer or iOS device that has Dropbox installed.

The procedure is identical for all cloud storage services.

Option 4: Utilize a remote backup

There are specific online backup options, such as Carbonite, which will backup your Mac over the web for a cost ($4.92 per month, 15-day free trial). The aforementioned cloud services are more for synchronizing and sharing files than keeping all your data. Another alternative is CrashPlan for Business ($9.99, 30-day free trial).

The advantage of one of these dedicated cloud backup services is that the backup is remote, so if your Mac was destroyed in a fire or flood along with your Time Machine backup, you would still have a copy of all your data in a secure facility (these places will have a way of keeping your data safe and accessible even if they suffer a power outage or something similar, although we're not sure about the end of the world scenarios).

If you have internet connectivity and your Mac crashes, gets lost or is stolen, you can recover everything from this cloud backup.

There was a less expensive alternative than hiring a business to host your backup. Previously, it was possible to use CrashPlan for Home to sync your data to a drive at a friend's house, which significantly reduced the cost. Unfortunately, this service is no longer available.

The primary downside of any of these techniques is that it can take a long time to complete the first backup of your data, particularly if you have a sluggish internet connection, and it can also take a long time to recover all of your data — it might take weeks to restore all of your data. If you upload or download several hundred terabytes of data, you may exceed the upload and download limits of your internet connection and incur additional costs. You may also search for a provider that will offer you a backup drive that you can then submit to them for storage.

How to back up your Mac to a cloud-based storage provider

As with the alternatives to Time Machine outlined above, the manner in which you back up your Mac to one of these online services will depend on which one you select; nonetheless, the procedure is likely to go as follows:

- Sign up for an account with the service; you may be required to sign up for a subscription rather than making a one-time payment, as is commonplace today.
- Install the supplier-supplied software and complete the setup procedure.
- There's a chance that the backup procedure will start instantly. This might take Very Considerable Time. There may be settings in the app's Preferences that allow you to speed up the backup process, albeit the majority of the backup speed is governed by your broadband connection.
- Examine what is being backed up and deselect any unnecessary items.
- When the worst comes and you need to recover your data you'll probably need to log in with your ID and password – so make sure you save a duplicate of them somewhere other than on the Mac you are backing up.

Option 5: Clone your hard drive

As with Time Machine, you may use the backup disk – or clone – to restore your Mac in the event of a failure and to recover a previous version of a document or a deleted photo. In addition, just as with Time Machine, you must remember to connect in your external hard drive for the backup.

A clone differs from a Time Machine backup in that it can be booted from, so you could connect it to another Mac and boot up from it without restoring your Mac, which may be handy as an interim solution. You cannot use Time Machine in this manner.

However, recovering your Mac from a clone is no longer as straightforward as it once was. Beginning with Catalina and concluding with Big Sur and the introduction of the M1 Mac, Apple's organization of startup volume has evolved over the previous few years. Apple now divides the drive in half, isolating writeable data from the system volume (which is read-only and is where all your system settings and all the things macOS needs to work are stored). Not only is this system volume read-only, but it is also sealed, which means that if the seal is broken – which will occur if you attempt to boot from an external drive – the volume will be invalidated.

There are several solutions that backup software makers have devised to circumvent this issue, but recovering a Mac from a backup is not as dependable as it previously was, not least because Apple might alter things again, rendering your bootable clone obsolete. So recovering from a clone is no longer the best approach to recovering your Mac following a calamity.

Nonetheless, the data volume may be backed up. To accomplish this, you could use Disk Utility to copy the Data volume to a disk image or a drive.

How to duplicate a Mac

The method you use to clone your Mac will depend on the software you are using to back up your Mac, the Mac you own, and the version of macOS it is running – it may not be possible at all – but if your Mac is capable of creating a clone, you can expect something like the following:

- Connect your external storage device.
- You may need to format, or reformat, the drive before you can use it. In this scenario, launch Disk Utility, pick the external drive, click Erase, select macOS Extended (Journaled) from the list of available formats, then click Erase again.
- Launch your cloning program.
- It's possible that the program will give you an option to 'Copy' what's on your Mac's internal storage to the external disk. You will need to be mindful of what you may replicate - ensure that you copy all files, for example, otherwise your clone may not be bootable.
- Before the copy begins, you may be required to provide a password and confirm that you wish to delete all data from the external device.
- Expect the cloning process to take some time; when it is complete, click OK.

The Genius Bar for Troubleshooting your Mac

The Apple Store is a wonderful place to purchase Apple devices and accessories, but they may also assist with inquiries and repairs. The Genius Bar at the Apple Store is the official location to receive hardware-related support for Apple devices.

Let's examine how to schedule an appointment with the Genius Bar the next time you need one.

What Can the Genius Bar of Apple Help With?

The Genius Bar offers assistance with all accessible Apple products. They may assist with queries and issues regarding hardware and software.

However, certain repairs cannot be performed in-store. The Genius Bar must send your device out for some extensive repairs and computer screen repairs. The majority of simple phone repairs, including battery and screen replacements, may be performed in-store and returned to you the same day.

What Can You Repair at Home Without an Apple Appointment?

Depending on the issue you are having, there are a few basic solutions you may attempt before scheduling an appointment at the Apple Genius Bar.

Reboot Your Equipment

Restarting your computer should be your first line of defense against the majority of software errors and performance concerns. If your iPhone or iPad is unresponsive, restart it forcefully.

To forcibly restart an iPhone 8 or later: press Volume Up and let it go, press Volume Down and let it go, and then push and hold down the Side button.

To forcibly restart an iPad without a home button, press and release the volume up and volume down buttons, and then press and hold the power button.

Hold down the power button to forcibly restart a Mac.

Run Mac Diagnostics

If a conventional restart doesn't work, you can try rebooting your Mac in diagnostic mode by holding down the D key when you switch it back on. Your Mac will test its functionality and provide a diagnostic code that describes the problem.

Address Common Overheating Causes

If your laptop is overheating, there are a handful of fast remedies that could help. Adjust your surroundings, dismiss demanding tabs or apps, check the activity monitor, or reset the fan. If your phone is overheating, transfer it to a cool spot. In the summer, iPhones frequently overheat when left in hot automobiles or exposed to excessive direct sunlight.

Check Your Battery Health

Battery repairs are one of the most common fixes needed for Apple products. Check the health of your iPhone or MacBook battery to determine if it's time to replace the battery.

How to Book an Apple Genius Bar Appointment

Once you've established that you actually need to bring your device into the Genius Bar, follow these steps to book an appointment:

- Visit Apple.com on your computer or mobile device.
- Select the Support option from the main menu.
- Choose Apple Repair
- Select Start a Maintenance Request
- Select the type of equipment for which you require an appointment. Select the category (iPhone, iPad, Watch, etc.) followed by the device model.

The website will highlight many kinds of device-related concerns. Choose the issue you're experiencing.

The site will then provide the option to send in the device, locate a nearby approved service provider, or schedule an appointment at the Genius Bar. To schedule an appointment with the Genius Bar, choose "Bring In For Repair."

It'll ask you for the serial number of the device if relevant, or to choose the device from the registered devices on your Apple account. If you need assistance discovering the serial number for any Apple product, please see our tutorial.

The site will now provide venues nearby where you can bring your device. To assist you in deciding where to go, their earliest appointment availability is displayed.

Choose your preferred Apple Store location and available appointment time from the list provided.

Resolve Problems with Your Apple Device by Scheduling an Appointment

The Genius Bar is an excellent resource for resolving Apple hardware issues. There is a multitude of repair methods for typical issues such as cracked displays and dead batteries. The Genius Bar can assist, but many customers prefer to perform repairs themselves or visit local businesses. Consider the risks and benefits of each alternative.

Bonus: Mac Keyboard Shortcut

I'm sure the majority of Mac users are aware that Command-C means copy and Command-V means paste, but there are a multitude of additional shortcuts that make life easier for Mac users. I've compiled the following examples to show this truth:

Esc

Never underestimate the Esc key's ability to get you out of trouble. Say you're taking a screenshot and managed to choose the part of your screen for that shot, only to learn it's the wrong section - touch Esc and you won't need to worry about it. That is essentially the Esc principle. Use it to cancel a prior command. Another example is a web page won't load and is sucking up your system resources?

Command-W

Closes the window that is presently active. Option-Command-W closes all active application windows.

Command-Y

Numerous individuals utilize QuickLook to preview products they are interested in. To utilize QuickLook, pick an item in the Finder and hit the space bar to display a preview. Select an item (you can even use the Up and Down arrows to navigate to it in Finder view) and then press Command-Y.

Command – Period (,)

This is one of the lesser-known Mac keyboard shortcuts, but it's really handy. You are working on an application, and you wish to see the application's preferences. You may browse to the menu bar and scroll through to view the preferences if you so want. Alternatively, you can press Command-, (comma) to access them as quickly as possible.

Command-G

I am certain that you utilize Command-F to locate objects, such as words in a document or on a website. Command-G is its lesser-known cousin. Utilize it to traverse through each occurrence of the desired object. This implies that if you use Command-F to locate all instances of "Command" on this page and then press Command-G, you may traverse through each one. Oh, and you can also press Shift-Command-G to return to the previous screen.

Command-M

This combination minimizes the front application window to the Dock, whereas Command-Option-M minimizes all front application windows.

Option and Direction

If you cannot view your desktop for all the open programs, click anywhere on your desktop while holding down Command and Option. You may just wish to access all open windows for a certain application; in this instance, hold down the same keys and click on any open window for that application.

Command-Shift-A

Select this combination when in Finder/Desktop view to access the Applications folder, or substitute the A with U to reach the Utility folder (or D for Desktop, H for Home, or I to access iCloud Drive).

Command-Space

The combination of Command-Space activates Spotlight; simply press and hold these keys and begin entering your query. (I suppose you already know about Command-tab?)

Command-L

The quickest method to do a search or browse to a website in Safari, Command-L quickly chooses the address bar: begin entering your query, then use the up/down arrows to select the right option.

Command-Tab

While holding down Command, launch the program switcher and use Tab to browse to the desired application.

Command-Option-D

Show or hide the dock from most applications.

Fn-left arrow (or right arrow)

Using the function key and the right (to the bottom of the page) or left (to the top of the page) arrows, you may quickly go to the top or bottom of a web page. You can accomplish the same result by pressing Command-Up or Command-Down. Utilize Control-Tab and Control-Shift-Tab as a third option.

Command-left/right arrows

Hit Command and the left arrow to go back to a page in the browser window. Press Command Right to continue going.

Tab nav

Use the Command-Shift-] and Command-Shift-[characters to navigate between different tabs.

Command-Shift-\

The simplest way to view all open tabs is within a single Safari window.

Option-Shift-Volume

Option Shift plus volume up/down allows you to adjust Mac's volume in tiny increments. Option Shift may also be used to adjust the display's brightness by tiny increments. Learn further Option secrets here.

Fn twice

To launch Dictation on your Mac, press the function (fn) key twice, then begin speaking, and press fn again when you're finished. Here are some additional suggestions for using your voice to control your Mac. Nota bene: macOS Catalina now includes the significantly more potent Voice Control, which allows you to control everything on your Mac using only your voice. Learn more about this topic here.

Option-File

Option when choosing the File menu in Safari provides access to the 'Close Other Tabs' command. Try the other Safari menu items with Option depressed to find other commands you probably weren't aware of.

Optional Brightness Boost (or down)

Utilize this command to launch preferences fast. Or, press Option in conjunction with the Mission Control or Volume (up/down) buttons to access the Mission Control and Sounds preferences.

Command – Backslash

This is one of the lesser-known Mac keyboard shortcuts, but it's really handy. Use this combination to navigate between open windows in the active application. You'll wonder why you hadn't utilized it earlier.

Command - Control - Space

Want to include emoji and other symbols in your writing? Control-Command-Space will bring up the Character Viewer, where you can select and use these symbols.

Command-P

Do you open a document before printing it using the File menu? Do this instead: Select the document in Finder and click Command-P. The item will open, and the Print dialogue will display. You may also use Command-P to print the current item in the majority of applications.

Option + Command + Esc

In the event that an application freezes or hangs, you can force quit it by pressing Option-Command-Esc. Sometimes, a simple program restart is all that's required to get your system back up and running.

Command + Management + Q

Leaving behind your Mac? Tap this keyboard shortcut to lock your computer immediately.

Touch Bar hint number 1

If you use a MacBook Pro with the Touch Bar, you may press Shift-Command-6 to grab a picture of what is on your Touch Bar. Want to get a picture to insert into the document you're typing in? Simply press Control-Option-Command-6, and the image will be copied to the clipboard.

Touch Bar tip No. 2

This MacBook Pro Touch Bar hint is especially helpful if you frequently hit the Siri button by accident: you can alter the button's location so you are less likely to do so. Choose to customize the control strip in Keyboard Preferences. Observe the Touch Bar, and you will notice that the icons are slightly unsettled. Move your pointer to the bottom of your screen and continue going (as if you were moving it off the screen); one of the touch bar items should be highlighted. Now, put your pointer on the Siri button and then drag and drop it a couple of spaces to the left.

Touch Bar hint number 3

Utilize the function keys often in some applications. Obviously, you may access them by hitting the 'fn' key. However, the Touch Bar may be configured to always display the function keys in such apps. To accomplish this, visit Keyboard System Preferences, choose Function Keys, and press the plus sign (+). Then you may choose the app (s). If you wish to perform a standard Control Strip command while using one of the applications, just press Fn to return to that view.

Safari tips

There are several keyboard shortcuts for Safari:

- Command + I: Open a new email message with the page's content.
- Command + Shift + I: Open a new email containing merely a page's URL.
- To shift your window down one screen, use the spacebar.
- Shift+Spacebar: Moves the window one screen higher.
- Command + Y: Open/close the History window.
- Option + Shift + T

This online browser trick can sometimes be a lifeline. When conducting research, Command + Shift + T will open your last closed tab, which is quite useful if you accidentally close a window without preserving the UR.

<u>Conclusion</u>

It is not a secret that the elderly are getting more tech-savvy and gaining access to the same technologies as the younger generation. The most recent Office of National Statistics (ONS) report on internet usage revealed that the number of older people using the internet has continued to rise, with 47% of those over the age of 75 and 83% of those between the ages of 65 and 74 being recent users.

So, it's excellent that a growing number of elderly individuals have realized the potential of computers and the internet. However, it is important to keep in mind that elderly users may require more assistance with setting up and maintaining their computers—and this is where local technical support comes into play.

<u>Are Macs superior for the elderly?</u>

We won't revisit the old Mac vs. PC discussion in this article, but there are several reasons why Macs are a great option for older users:

- They are simpler to install.
- They're easier and more intuitive to use
- They're more protected
- They sync effortlessly with other Apple gadgets including iPhones, iPad, HomeKit, and other devices
- Their integrated software is perfect for simple picture and video editing. Many customers choose Macs because of their satisfaction with the Apple ecosystem, which makes it simple

to attach their iPhone or Apple TV to their Mac for file sharing and content synchronization. For older users, it makes sense to stay within one ecosystem to avoid confusion and compatibility difficulties, but help may still be required on occasion.:

Nowadays, we use our smartphones for almost everything except when it comes to picking a phone for the elderly. As a result, narrowing down your key goals is beneficial.

Furthermore, determining how your elderly will use their phones will assist you in selecting a model as well as a voice and data package. As a result, the following are the most typical cases for seniors to use Iphone:

- Making phone calls in an emergency
- Texting with relatives and friends
- Video calling friends and relatives
- Considering the date and time
- Managing your smart gadgets (like a smart thermostat or smart lock)
- Using GPS to assist with navigation when driving or walking
- On-the-go weather checking Monitoring health via apps
- Using the internet

Nowadays, the use of smartphones has increased to the point that it appears that everyone owns one. Indeed, 42% of people aged 65 and older already own cellphones, up from 18% in 2013.

Furthermore, Internet use and home broadband adoption have increased significantly among this population. Today, 67% of seniors utilize the internet, a significant rise from 12% a little under two decades ago.

There are some features on mobile phones that were made just for seniors and can make it much easier for them to use the device. Here are a few examples of senior-friendly cell phone features:

- Full Keyboards and Simple Menus
- Internet Connection
- Larger Buttons and Displays
- Options with a Higher Volume
- Voice Typing and Voiceover Capabilities
- Magnifying Glasses
- Timers, Alerts, and Alarms
- Button of Emergency
- GPS Fitness and Health Tracking Applications

I trust that after reading this book you feel comfortable with all the subjects covered and that you find using your iPhone and MacBook to be a lot less daunting.

Made in the USA
Las Vegas, NV
09 January 2023

65242142R00148